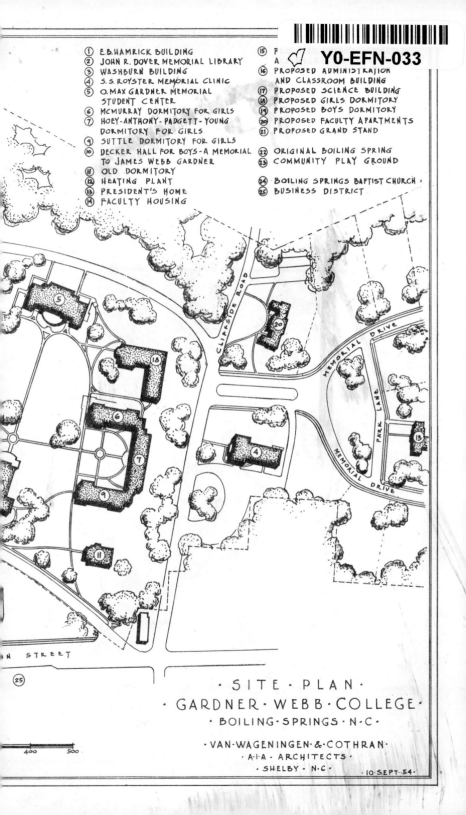

YO-EFN-033

① E.B. HAMRICK BUILDING
② JOHN R. DOVER MEMORIAL LIBRARY
③ WASHBURN BUILDING
④ S.S. ROYSTER MEMORIAL CLINIC
⑤ O. MAX GARDNER MEMORIAL STUDENT CENTER
⑥ MCMURRAY DORMITORY FOR GIRLS
⑦ HOEY-ANTHONY-PADGETT-YOUNG DORMITORY FOR GIRLS
⑨ SUTTLE DORMITORY FOR GIRLS
⑩ DECKER HALL FOR BOYS - A MEMORIAL TO JAMES WEBB GARDNER
⑪ OLD DORMITORY
⑫ HEATING PLANT
⑬ PRESIDENT'S HOME
⑭ FACULTY HOUSING

⑮ ...
⑯ PROPOSED ADMINISTRATION AND CLASSROOM BUILDING
⑰ PROPOSED SCIENCE BUILDING
⑱ PROPOSED GIRLS DORMITORY
⑲ PROPOSED BOYS DORMITORY
⑳ PROPOSED FACULTY APARTMENTS
㉑ PROPOSED GRAND STAND

㉒ ORIGINAL BOILING SPRING
㉓ COMMUNITY PLAY GROUND

㉔ BOILING SPRINGS BAPTIST CHURCH
㉕ BUSINESS DISTRICT

CLIFFSIDE ROAD

MEMORIAL DRIVE

PARK LANE

MEMORIAL DRIVE

N STREET

400   500

· SITE · PLAN ·
· GARDNER · WEBB · COLLEGE ·
· BOILING · SPRINGS · N · C ·

· VAN · WAGENINGEN · & · COTHRAN ·
· A·I·A · ARCHITECTS ·
· SHELBY · N·C ·

· 10 · SEPT · 54 ·

OLIVER MAX GARDNER
(1882–1947)

Lengthened Shadows:

A HISTORY OF GARDNER-WEBB COLLEGE

1907-1956

LENGTHENED SHADOWS:

1957

BOILING SPRINGS

Francis B. Dedmond

A HISTORY OF
GARDNER-WEBB COLLEGE
1907-1956

GARDNER-WEBB COLLEGE

To

Mrs. J. D. Huggins, Sr.

who loved the school

in the beginning

and

who loves it

still.

Contents

Preface

THIS IS the story of a school, as Governor O. Max Gardner put it in 1942, that "refused to die," even though at times there were those even among its friends who were no doubt convinced that a *coup de grace* would have indeed been an act of kindness. Especially was this true during the bleak, depression-ridden 1930's when the institution was kept alive through the dogged determination, faith, and sacrifice of faithful friends, trustees, and faculty. This is the story of the growth and struggle and struggle and growth of Gardner-Webb College from its beginning as a denominational high school to the end of the College's academic year 1955-1956.

James Boswell quotes Dr. Samuel Johnson as having said that "Great abilities are not requisite for an historian; for in historical composition, all the greatest powers of the human mind are quiescent. He has facts ready to his hand, so there is no exercise of invention. Imagination is not required in any great degree; only about as much as is used in the lower kinds of poetry. Some penetration, accuracy, and coloring will fit a man for the task, if he can give the application which is necessary."

I am willing to grant Dr. Johnson his major premise. All the facts, however, an author might wish are not always available. When the Memorial Building burned in

1937, many of the records that this author could have wished "ready to his hand" during the writing of this history went up in smoke. Meager indeed were the source materials for some of the early years of this history. Perhaps even Dr. Johnson, had he known the number of historians likely to be faced with such a situation, would not have discounted so readily the value of the gift of "historical" invention and a fertile imagination in the historian. I have attempted to sprinkle a little coloring here and there. I hope, however, that the accuracy of this history has not been distorted by the coloring nor the coloring dimmed by the accuracy.

There are several persons to whom I am indebted, in one way or another, for help in the preparation of this history—persons who have reduced the amount of application the author had to give to his task. To Mrs. Dorothy Washburn Hamrick am I indebted for the compilation and statistics of the appendices. Mrs. Bessie Atkins Huggins supplied the author with a lot of material relative to the Boiling Springs High School period—a period in the school's history that she knows better than any living person. I am indebted to Mrs. Hubert C. Dixon not only for typing the manuscript, but for her suggestions, stylistic and otherwise, which have improved the story I set out to tell. I owe a debt of gratitude also to Mrs. Betty Barker Norris, a former secretary of mine, and to Miss Wilma Moxley for their aid in helping me compile the notes from which this book was written. Many others, to be sure,—Mr. Joe C. Washburn, President Phil Elliott, Miss Abbie Miller, Professor Hubert C. Dixon, Dr. Wyan Washburn, the Reverend J. L. Jenkins, Vice-President Lawson Allen, and others I shall not list here—also had a part in making possible the writing of this history of Gardner-Webb College.

F. B. D.
BOILING SPRINGS, NORTH CAROLINA
OCTOBER 30, 1956

Introduction

RALPH WALDO EMERSON said in his essay "Self-Reliance" that "An institution is the lengthened shadow of one man." There may be, to be sure, some institutions to which Emerson's dictum applies *in toto*. However, I doubt if there is or ever has been a college that reached its Golden Anniversary year to which Emerson's declaration can be applied with any degree of literalness. We can, however, paraphrase his well-known epigrammatic statement and arrive at, I believe, a fair generalization as to what a college is: "A college is the lengthened shadows of many men and women." At least, there can be little doubt but that such is true of Gardner-Webb College. It is today figuratively the shadows of Professor J. D. Huggins, Miss Etta Curtis, Governor O. Max Gardner, President Phil Elliott, and a host of others transfigured into ideals and attitudes as well as into brick and mortar. This is the *raison d'etre* for the title LENGTHENED SHADOWS, which this semi-centennial history of Gardner-Webb College bears.

Gardner-Webb College is a Christian liberal arts junior college; and as such, it shares with all other Christian liberal arts colleges those basic concepts that make colleges of this type unique among institutions of higher learning. First of all, such colleges are unique because Christianity itself is unique among the religions of the world. In Christianity in a unique way, the eternal God has been revealing Himself to finite man. In the Christian revelation God Himself entered into the stream of human history and is still making Himself known to man. It is desirable, therefore, that Christians understand a great deal about the institutions, the social, political, and economic forces and ideologies, and the cultural and esthetic values of the civilization in which God is making Himself known. Only the Christian liberal arts college is designed definitely and avowedly to accomplish this purpose.

Secondly, Gardner-Webb and other Christian liberal arts colleges are unique among the institutions of higher learning because they are predicated upon three assumptions concerning the nature of man: Man is regarded as a rational being—a creature of mind—who finds himself in a universe of which he desires to make sense; man is regarded as a moral being who, in his best moments, desires the good life and who is ever and anon faced with making moral judgments; and man is regarded as a spiritual being whose destiny is of a transcendent nature—transcending both the physical universe and time.

The term "liberal arts" means literally "the arts becoming to a free man." The subject matter of genuine liberal arts colleges will be such as will increase the freedom of the mind and free man—free him from himself, from his prejudices, his preconceived notions, and his worthless devotions. President John Sloan Dickey of Dartmouth College said that "the American liberal arts college can find a significant, even unique mission in the duality of its historic purpose: to see men made whole in *both* competence and conscience." President Nathan M. Pusey of Harvard declared that the liberal arts colleges have come from "an ancient, broad, and deep tradition of mind and spirit. Nurtured in adventure, boldness, and fresh vision, they have always recognized at their best that their responsibil-

ity is not to minister to utility but rather to call men to
moral and spiritual, and to intellectual responsibility." The
liberal arts will help man assess the validity of the *Zeitgeist*
by bringing him into contact with the ideas and ideals
which have made Western culture what it is. The liberal
arts, then,—religion, literature, philosophy, language, history, the fine arts, the natural sciences, and the others—
are not unproductive disciplines because their value cannot be calculated on an IBM machine. Rather they are
productive disciplines because they help to prepare man
for his greatest adventure and most satisfying experience—
the living of a free and noble life.

The very essence of Western culture—the warp of the
fabric—is the Judaeo-Christian tradition. Thus, Western
culture can be understood only in the light of Christianity.
It is the mission, then, of Gardner-Webb College and other
Christian liberal arts colleges to educate the liberal man
and woman in a Christian atmosphere, where the Author
of All Truth is reverenced and where liberating truth, both
spiritual and intellectual, is sought and taught.

It should be pointed out, however, that a Christian liberal arts college is not a Christian college because its curriculum is necessarily different from that of a non-Christian college; but unlike the non-Christian college, it has
a different perspective from which it sees and evaluates its
curriculum. However, any liberal arts college—whether
church-related or publicly supported—is an intellectual
institution which, whatever else it does, must seek the
expansion and perfection of the intellects of its students.
It must endeavor to open the minds of its students, to
enable them to comprehend, to give the mind, as John
Henry Newman said, "power, flexibility, sagacity, and elo-
quence of expression." The mind should be trained so that
it can "reach out toward truth." This never means simply
the cultivation of the memory, for the mere storing up
of facts and figures, scolia and schemata, without thought
upon them is of relatively little value. The true expansion
and perfection of the mind comes "in the action of the

mind upon knowledge," in seeing relationships, in comparing one idea with another, and in seeing the whole in the part and understanding the harmony of the parts. All this, as Newman pointed out, leads to philosophy, which is simply knowledge illuminated by thought until principles are seen and comprehended. The end product, then, of Christian liberal arts education is the philosophic mind in the maturing Christian. Dante said that philosophy ". . . has as its subject understanding, and as its form an almost divine love of the thing understood." The philosophic mind has the ability to fall in love with the thing understood and to experience the ecstasy of learning.

But Gardner-Webb College not only shares with other Christian liberal arts colleges certain common ideals and objectives, but it is also, in one particular respect, different from most, so different, in fact, as to be almost unique. I refer to its community-service concept. When President Phil Elliott assumed the presidency of the College in 1943, he brought with him some deep-seated and definite ideas concerning the service a college ought to render to its area. It should attempt, in so far as it reasonably can, to minister to the intellectual, physical, cultural, religious, and recreational needs of the people. It should offer its services to the agricultural, business, and industrial interests of the area. With these ideals in mind, Gardner-Webb College fashioned its Church-Community Development program, developed the program of its Guidance Department, and built and staffed the Gardner-Webb Community Health Center. And less than an hour before the writing of this Introduction was begun, President Elliott informed the author that the contract had been let for the new Gardner-Webb College Recreation Center, a building to meet the athletic, physical education, and recreational needs of the College's students, but a building also which is to double as a recreation center for the community as well.

The thinking back of Gardner-Webb's community-service concept is in line with the best thinking being done concerning the expanding role and basic function of community colleges. Jesse Parker Bogue in his book, THE COMMUNITY COLLEGE, says that when the President's Commission on Higher Education used the term "community college," it had in mind an institution, the first qualification of which is "*service* primarily to the people of the community." The community college should, according to Mr. Bogue, attempt "to meet the needs of the people in the broadest cultural aspects as well as the vocational." The activities of the college should be integrated to the fullest possible degree with the activities of the community and should be the center for the administration of a comprehensive adult education program.

With these basic concepts, Gardner-Webb College is in agreement. However, Gardner-Webb is not a community college as the term is normally used, but is a liberal arts college with a community-service concept. In three important aspects, Gardner-Webb is different from the ordinary community college. The first is the manner of its *control*. Most community colleges are controlled by a board of trustees elected by the people or appointed by some elected official or officials of the state or community-college district. Gardner-Webb's Board of Trustees is approved by the North Carolina Baptist State Convention. The second difference is the manner of *financial support*. Community colleges look to the state for direct appropriations or to the communities for current funds from monies provided for by taxation. Gardner-Webb receives no support from taxation or from the public coffers. Yet it renders services to the community at large, services toward which the people have not contributed through taxation. The third difference is one of *emphasis*. Many community colleges are largely vocational. While Gardner-Webb does offer some terminal vocational education, it is predominantly a liberal arts college. In short, Gardner-Webb is a private college that wishes to use its resources to serve all of its area in reasonable and feasible ways to the end that the educational, physical, cultural, economic, recreational, and religious levels and tone may be raised and the welfare and well-being of the people enhanced.

But President Phil Elliott stoutly maintains that the community-service concept of education in privately controlled and supported Gardner-Webb College is not his "greatest good," as he put it, to the College. President Elliott feels that his being able through the years to secure for the College a worthy faculty is his most significant contribution. Bricks and mortar and a well-stocked library do not make a school. These simply provide the facilities and the tools for the use of consecrated teachers in the rewarding task of seeking to develop cultured and cultivated individuals of the students who enroll at Gardner-Webb. Alas, however, those who have, through the years, done most to make the College what it was and is—the past and present faculty—are not accorded, even in a history such as this, their proper place in the *dramatis personae*. They were largely unsung and thus largely unchronicled. They went about their tasks, but did not get into the sources of this story of the College. The historian does not want to write only about kings and potentates, but often he can not find out what those who gave meaning to the kings and potentates were about. Thus the chronicler of this story pleads *non abstante aliquo statuo in contrarium.*

PROFESSOR JAMES DWYRE HUGGINS, SR.
(1874-1932)

The Past Is Prologue

SINCE shortly after the Civil War, the Baptists of the Kings Mountain Association in west-central North Carolina have shown an unusual interest in education, both in higher education and in that offered by the academies and high schools. In the 1873 Report on Education, read to the Association at Zion Church, young ministers were urged "to avail themselves of [the] opportunity provided" at Wake Forest College. The Association was also reminded of the Bridges Academy at Boiling Springs. The Report the following year at Sandy Run Church announced that "schoolhouses are being built in several locations; one has just been completed on our line near the Burnt Chimneys, . . .; another on Buffalo [Creek], near Capernaum Church, and others in other sections." In 1875 the Association met at New Hope Church, and the Committee on Education recommended that Wake Forest College and the various schools "in our midst, such as Burnt Chimneys and Shelby Academy" be supported.

By the late 1870's, a "female college" was being planned for Shelby. In 1880 R. E. Porter reported to the Kings Mountain Association, meeting at Double Springs Church, that "the time has come when we must educate. It is a religious duty and cannot be ignored," and the next year H. W. Reinhardt urged the Association to educate girls as well as boys. In 1882, the Association met at Bethel Church in Rutherford County on September 20. At that time it was announced that "the Shelby Baptist Church had a first-class female college in operation, . . . The college was under the management of Elder R. D. Mallary, late president of Shorter College of Rome, Georgia. He added to his corps of teachers those equal to the best in the land."

The financial burden of supporting such a college proved rather grievous to the Shelby Church, and the institution was not destined to last long. In 1885, at the meeting of the Association at State Line Church, Grover, N. C., it was reported that the "Shelby Church and other churches and individuals have supported the female college for three years, and now the committee asks that the Association adopt it as their [sic] own daughter." Two years later President Mallary resigned "from the female college on account of ill health," and E. J. Willis of Virginia was elected to replace him. The College was not mentioned in the reports to the Association after 1888. In fact, in 1889 the Association was told that "the Judson College at Hendersonville was the only Baptist school then, where the girls had the same educational advantages as the boys." The fact that this statement appears in the *Minutes* and the fact that no mention was made in 1889 of the Shelby Female College seem to indicate that the College closed before the 1889 Associational meeting.

The Kings Mountain Association time and again "remembered" Wake Forest College. When the Association met at Pleasant Grove Church in 1883, efforts were then being made to raise a $100,000 endowment for Wake Forest. The Association indicated its desire to give $2000. The depression of 1893 threatened to close Wake Forest, and the leaders of the Kings Mountain Association were concerned, especially since Wake Forest was a center for the education of Baptist ministers. In 1895, the Association was told "that the first object of the Baptist Constitution is to help poor but promising preachers to prepare themselves for the ministry." The property at Wake Forest, the Association was reminded, "is just as much ours as it is those who live near the college."

At this same 1895 meeting hope was expressed "that our female college at Raleigh will open in '96." The 1897 report of the Committee on Education of the Kings Mountain Association mentioned "the progress of our female university at Raleigh." "We hope," the Committee stated, "within the near future to give the girls the same advantages there as the boys have at Wake Forest." The Baptist Female University did not open until September, 1899. The name was changed to the Baptist University for Women in 1905 and to Meredith College in 1909.

In the late 1890's the Association became more and more interested in local schools. The Education Committee in 1896 mentioned the "high school at Cleveland Mills, being taught by W. B. Dove, this being in our midst." At the same time the Committee recommended "a good high school in every association in the state as feeders of our Baptist colleges." In 1900 the Education Committee declared "that the time has now come for the education of all the people, as well as the ministers . . ." The next year the Committee pleaded for Christian education and for the establishment of Baptist schools in the Kings Mountain Association. "Whom shall we leave here," the Committee asked, "to advocate and defend our faith, the principles we hold so dear, as against the attacks of those who reject them, if we fail to teach our children?" Two years later the Committee again stressed the need for more Baptist high schools, pointing out that there was "too great a step from our common schools to our colleges." The report continued: "While conceding the right and duty of the State to provide common school education, we must regard the various Christian denominations as in duty bound to make provisions for the higher education of their own adherents and to exert a positive influence in such education. For this purpose some of our sister associations have established and are maintaining associational high schools. Your Committee would therefore recommend that a special committee be appointed to investigate the matter of building a Baptist high school in our association or in connection with our neighboring association."

With the appointment of this investigating committee at the 1903 meeting of the Kings Mountain Association at Pleasant Hill Church, the history of Gardner-Webb College actually has its beginning. The committee was composed of the Reverend J. V. Devenny, Chairman A. C. Irvin, J. E. McBrayer, D. F. Putnam, and A. H. Sims. The committee reported at the next session of the Association, which convened at Zoar Church in September, 1904, in favor of an associational high school and recommended that a Board of fifteen Trustees be appointed at once.

The Trustees were to be grouped into three classes—the first class to serve one year; the second class, two years; and the third class, three years. The committee recommended that W. W. Washburn, L. S. Jenkins, G. W. Kendrick, J. M. Wilson, and the Reverend J. V. Devenny be elected to the first class of Trustees; that E. C. Borders, J. H. Quinn, A. T. Mull, G. H. Logan, and A. C. Irvin be elected to the second class; and that Carme Elam, E. B. Hamrick, N. B. Kendrick, L. S. Hamrick, and D. F. Putnam be elected to the third class. The Trustees, the committee recommended, were to act as representatives of the Association; they were to acquire property, collect and administer funds, select a site and erect buildings for the school, employ and dismiss teachers, exercise all other duties exercised by such bodies, and at an early date procure from the State of North Carolina a charter for the school. The Association adopted the recommendations and began to receive subscriptions for the school.

On October 10, 1904, the Trustees met in the First Baptist Church of Shelby. The Reverend J. V. Devenny was elected Chairman and Carme Elam was elected Secretary. The Trustees also appointed Mr. Devenny as Financial Agent of the Board to solicit funds. At the meeting on January 10, 1905, by-laws were adopted; and on March 1, J. H. Quinn was elected Treasurer of the Board.

The prospects of a denominational high school created a lot of interest, especially as to where it would be located. Several communities wanted the school. The Board scheduled a meeting for May 8, 1905, to receive propositions from the communities seeking the school. On Saturday, two days before the meeting, the Boiling Springs Baptist Church called a conference. J. Y. Hamrick made a motion that the church offer the old church house and two acres of land with the understanding that, if the school should later have to close, the land would be given back to the church. He also made a motion that the church appoint a committee of five to take a subscription and appear before the Trustees in Shelby on the following Monday. The church accepted the motions and appointed A. J. Green, A. R. Hamrick, J. Y. Hamrick, Noah Hamrick, and John Green to represent the church at the Shelby meeting.

The Boiling Springs committeemen went to Shelby in a buggy. While they were in the meeting, some children evidently played in the buggy, for the men found a doll in the buggy when they came out of the meeting. They brought the doll back to Boiling Springs and reported, "We have brought the first student to the new school."

Their optimism proved to be well founded; however, it was not until two months later that the Board decided that the school would be built at Boiling Springs. Following the meeting on May 8, the Trustees appointed a special committee to visit the various communities seeking the school and to report back to the Board. The special committee filed its report and also, so it seems, allowed committees from the communities to present their claims before the Board. At this meeting on July 10, 1905, in the First Baptist Church of Shelby, Boiling Springs was chosen by the Board as the site for the new school. According to the *Cleveland Star*, July 12, 1905, "several flattering inducements were made, notably by Lawndale and El Bethel, but the offer of Boiling Springs and its convenient and suitable location made its selection the most desirable."

Boiling Springs, as a community, had long been interested in the education of its youth. By 1870 the Lovelace School, one-fourth of a mile from Sandy Run Creek, was in operation. At different times Professor B. H. Bridges and Professor D. S. Lovelace taught in this log schoolhouse. By 1873, Bridges Academy was attracting the notice of the people of the area; and from time to time the Committee on Education of the Kings Mountain Association mentioned the "good school" at Boiling Springs taught by B. H. Bridges. Another schoolhouse used at about the same time was known as the Holland Schoolhouse. It was located on what is now the Gardner-Webb College Farm. Professor Bridges, however, set to work to consolidate the Lovelace and Holland schools; and as a consequence of his efforts, a two-room schoolhouse was built where the present Boiling Springs School stands. It was known as the Boiling Springs Academy.

Professor B. H. Bridges has been called the "Father of Education" in the Boiling Springs community. He was responsible directly for much of the interest in education in Boiling Springs before the establishment of the denominational high school. Thus he was indirectly responsible and to him should go some of the credit for the school's being located at Boiling Springs. Most of his adult life was devoted to teaching, with the exception of a short time during which he practiced dentistry. Although he never went to college and was a man virtually self-taught, he is quoted as having said as far back perhaps as 1875: "One day there will be a college here." And a college ultimately there was. But first, a high school.

Even before that, however, there must be money. And it came, slowly to be sure, but it came. By the time the

Kings Mountain Association met on September 21, 1905, the Reverend J. V. Devenny, the Financial Agent, reported the total subscription, not including the local subscription at Boiling Springs, to be $1475.12.

At this session of the Association, a resolution by J. Y. Hamrick was unanimously adopted inviting the Sandy Run Association to join the Kings Mountain Association in erecting and operating the school which had been located near the border line of the two Associations. A committee, composed of the Reverend J. V. Devenny, J. Y. Hamrick, the Reverend C. J. Woodson, the Reverend A. C. Irvin, and R. L. Weathers, was appointed to meet with the Sandy Run Association at its October 1905 session and to present the resolution. For some time the Sandy Run Association had been attempting to establish a school, but without success. Nearly a year before—November 16, 1904—the following announcement appeared in the *Cleveland Star*: "Every church in the Sandy Run Association is requested to send one delegate to Bethel Church at Ellenboro on Friday, December 2, 1904, to make arrangements about our high school. Any inducements you may have to offer, please bring them along." The inducements were no doubt not alluring enough, not nearly so much so as the later offer of the Kings Mountain Association. Here was the easy yet practical way to get a school. And the Sandy Run Association "unanimously and enthusiastically accepted the invitation" and appointed ten Trustees to serve jointly with the fifteen from the Kings Mountain Association. They were W. A. Martin, Dr. T. G. Hamrick, T. M. Holland, A. S. Harrill, D. M. Harrill, Dr. T. B. Lovelace, J. H. Hamrick, J. J. Edwards, the Reverend J. M. Hamrick, and J. C. Bridges.

The Trustees held their first joint meeting at Boiling Springs on October 27, 1905, and adopted a plan of cooperation and a new set of by-laws. They decided that the school should be known as the Boiling Springs High School, and they appointed a committee, composed of J. H. Quinn, J. F. Alexander, and Carme Elam, to secure a charter. A second committee also was appointed to secure plans, which were to be submitted at the next meeting of the Board, for two wooden buildings.

The Trustees met next on November 13. The Building Committee submitted its plans for the two wooden structures, the cost of which was not to exceed $5000. However, the Board rejected these plans and decided to erect a brick building to cost $10,000, and another committee was appointed to carry out the decision of the Board.

According to the "Boiling Springs Church Minutes," February 3, 1906, the church acted upon a motion by R. H. Green to give to the school three and eight-tenths acres rather than the two that had been promised earlier. On April 27, the committee appointed to secure a charter reported that the charter had been secured and that the name of the school was to be Boiling Springs High School, Incorporated. The chairman of the committee also reported that the Boiling Springs Church had given the school a deed to the land it had promised to donate and that titles had also been secured to other land as well, amounting to a total of 8.6 acres.

A little over a month later—on June 1—the Board received the architect's drawings from J. M. McMichael. The drawings were approved; and shortly afterwards, the contract was let for the material. D. P. Queen, who was described as a successful contractor, was given the building contract. By the time the Kings Mountain Association met in the fall, the Association was told that the materials were "being secured and laid down on the grounds at Boiling Springs." On September 20, subscriptions had been received amounting to $6716.67, $2207.50 of which had already been collected.

N. B. Kendrick and his brothers were given the contract to make the bricks for what is now known as the Huggins-Curtis Building. The brick kiln was on the land of Mrs. J. L. Pruette, near the campus. Mrs. J. V. Devenny hauled the first load of bricks. Someone offered to help her; but she replied, "No, I'm going to do it myself." She hitched a horse to a one-horse wagon, drove to the brick kiln, loaded her wagon, hauled the bricks to the school site, and unloaded them herself. John F. Moore, early trustee and long-time friend of the school, was the first man to haul a load of bricks from the same kiln. His was a man-sized, two-horse wagon load.

The ground-breaking ceremony was held early in the spring of 1907. The pupils of the Boiling Springs Public School, as it was then called, along with their teachers— Miss Lizzie Elliott, Miss Euzelia Hamrick, and Miss Gertie Green—marched two abreast, with the smallest children in front, to the site of the new building. Esley Green, one of the pupils, beat the drum. R. H. Green, Sr., oldest charter member of the Boiling Springs Church (organized September 15, 1847), led the group. Mr. Green lifted the first shovel of dirt; Esley Green, the second; and Connie Green, the smallest little girl in the group and a first grader, the third. They were followed by every pupil, probably as many as a hundred, and the three teachers.

Work on the building started. In 1907, the Kings Mountain Association met at the Bessemer City Baptist Church at which time the Reverend J. V. Devenny submitted the Report of the Trustees of the High School. He stated that the Board met on January 1, 1907, and that at that time about $10,000 had been subscribed, an amount which seemed then to justify the action of the Board. Thus the Board unanimously instructed its Building Committee to proceed with the work according to the previous plans. The contractor agreed to erect the building at a total cost of $6000. The Committee was to furnish all material and the contractor to perform all necessary labor, and work on the building was started in the latter part of March under the direction of the Chairman of the Committee. The work, however, was stopped on May 25. At that time the Board found that funds on hand were not sufficient to buy the materials and meet the payrolls of the contractor. But the work must not remain stopped, the

Trustees felt; and so it was suggested that a joint note be
signed by members of the Board and a loan of $3000 be se-
cured to supplement money being collected in order that
a roof might be put on the building.

The loan was negotiated. About this time, J. D. Huggins, Sr., was hired as Field Agent until the school could
be opened. Mr. Huggins would then, so he understood,
be employed as a teacher. John F. Moore was appointed
to superintend the erection of the building so that the
Chairman of the Building Committee—Mr. Devenny—
might have time to handle his other duties as Financial
Agent. At another meeting on July 25, 1907, an additional
loan was arranged—this time for $5000. By the time a
report was submitted on September 20, the south wing of
the building was ready for the roof timbers, with an estimated 100,000 bricks yet to be laid on the walls of the
center and north wings. Subscriptions now amounted to
$10,824.34, with $6036.12 having already been collected.

At the same meeting of the Kings Mountain Association—that of 1907—the Committee on Education, composed of B. T. Falls, R. L. Weathers, and J. Y. Hamrick,
made a strong plea for support of the school at Boiling
Springs:

> Our secondary schools which have done such a great work for
> the denomination and for civilization are steadily growing in size
> and usefulness. We heartily commend them to all parents who
> desire to obtain for their children a Christian education. We fur-
> ther recommend and urge that it is the duty of every Baptist in
> this Association to lend to these schools their moral support and
> contribute their financial aid. We commend especially the main-
> tenance of the Boiling Springs High School, which is designed to
> meet the demands for better high school facilities. Your Com-
> mittee believes that there is a great work for this school to do and
> it should have an important place in our denominational work. It
> is designed to, and if supported, will do more to strengthen the
> Baptist cause in this Association than any other means now before
> us. To this end then let this Association pledge its united and
> most loyal support to the erection and maintenance of this school.
>
> While profoundly grateful for the progress made thus far, the
> goal is far in the distance. Our civilization, which is essentially

Christian, can be maintained in its purity and advanced only by the aid of a Christian education. Furthermore, the Church must educate in its own interest, for the work is great and the laborers, if educated, are equal to the task. Our denominational schools are the only means by which our public life can be supplied with the true interpretation of the Christian view of the world, which best conserves the state and civilization. Believing then as we do that the welfare of our denomination depends upon the usefulness and efficiency of our educational system, we would urge upon this Association that they continue to give to our schools that loyal support and liberal patronage which has enabled them to prosper in the past.

The cornerstones—one for each of the two sponsoring Associations—were laid on June 29, 1907. In order to seat the large crowd that came for the ceremony, an outdoor bleacher was built of rough lumber. A speaker's platform was also made of the same material. On the speaker's platform that day were the Reverend J. V. Devenny, J. Y. Hamrick, Professor J. D. Huggins, J. H. Quinn, and Dr. Edwin McNeill Poteat, President of Furman University and speaker for the occasion. Mr. Devenny presided; J. H. Quinn delivered the welcome address; and J. Y. Hamrick introduced the speaker. Dr. Poteat's address, so far as is known, has not been preserved. It, however, has been described as "a masterly one." Following the address, several articles were deposited in each cornerstone: a Bible, the school's charter, copies of the Kings Mountain and Sandy Run Association *Minutes* of 1906, the Cleveland County paper and the Rutherford County paper, and some money. The Reverend J. M. Hamrick led in the closing prayer.

Boiling Springs was described in the first catalogue of the school as a community "isolated from the allurements surrounding a city or a railroad town . . . [and] free from those vices and temptations that lead the young from the paths of rectitude." The second catalogue described the community as a "quiet country place . . . free from the allurements of city or town life; and the temptations to vice and idleness, found in more densely populated sections, are not met with. Nevertheless, surrounded as it is by an intelligent and cultured citizenship, it has all the social pleasures and recreation that can, with safety, be thrown around young men and women." There were two wooden stores in this "quiet country place." The Masonic Order met over McSwain's Store. The blacksmith shop was next to the public school. A cotton gin stood where the Co-Ed Theatre now stands. Boiling Springs also had a roller mill and a saw mill; and, after the school came, Boiling Springs got back its post office, which the R.F.D. had killed some time before.

The Boiling Springs Church, to be sure, was not unmindful of the part it must play if the school were to succeed in accomplishing the purpose for which it was founded. The "Boiling Springs Church Minutes" contain a resolution passed by the deacons in October of 1907. It pointed to the fact that "the eyes of the members of the 69 churches in the Kings Mountain and Sandy Run Associations are turned upon us" and that "these churches are piling up their money at our door and sending their sons and daughters among us for literary and spiritual training." With the school came "new opportunities and new obligations." The deacons, therefore, resolved that they would "endeavor to maintain the standards of morality and religion of this community and church as handed down by our forefathers."

At a meeting of the Board on July 25, 1907, J. D. Huggins, Sr., was chosen Principal of the school and was authorized to select a faculty. He was thirty-two years of age at the time. He was born in Kershaw County, near Camden, S. C., and had been brought up on a farm. When he was about fifteen years of age, one of his legs was injured; and for nearly a year, he had to remain in bed. For four years thereafter he was an invalid, but when he was able to be on crutches, he went back to school until he secured a teaching position near Lynchburg, S. C. Later, for a year, he attended Welsh Neck High School, now

Coker College, at Hartsville, S. C., and the following year, entered Catawba College, then located at Newton, N. C. Before he completed his college course, his leg began to trouble him again; and he went home for treatment. He later taught for one session near Clyde, S. C., before returning to college, where he worked at odd jobs to support himself. For instance, during his senior year, he gave Magic Lantern shows, accompanied by lectures. His leg, however, continued to give him trouble until he finally had to have an operation, which proved at least temporarily successful. This is the man who served as first Principal of Boiling Springs High School and first Dean of Boiling Springs College and who was affectionately known as "Professor" Huggins. So completely was Professor Huggins identified with the school in the thinking of students and others that the *Kalarathea*, the college newspaper, in 1929 declared that "it is impossible for anyone to understand or even imagine all that must be meant when we say 'Professor Huggins and Boiling Springs High School and College.' When we speak of this school, we invariably think of it as a group or institution with Professor Huggins as father."

2

Boiling Springs High School— 1907-1928

Professor Huggins secured a faculty; the students came, 135 that first year, with Carl Edwards being the first to enroll. Only the building was not ready. But the school opened anyway in October of 1907. The students were housed in various homes in the community. Tommy Goode had recently built a six-room house for himself, but he let twelve girls and Miss Lula McGee, the Lady Principal, occupy the house until the new building was ready. Other students and faculty members were placed in homes near-by.

The first faculty consisted of Professor Huggins, Miss Lula McGee, Miss Alma Smith, Miss Annie Hamrick, and Miss Mary Clarke Pitts. The faculty and students met together for the first time in the old public school building—a wooden building of only three rooms. Many of the community people also were present, although some could not be seated. A Scripture passage was read; prayer was offered; and brief talks were made by the Reverend J. V.

Devenny, J. Y. Hamrick, and Professor Huggins. Classes
were then organized.

Since the public school, at that time, was in session only
three months during the winter, the school Trustees allowed the new school to use the three rooms of the building until January, 1908. The school, however, did not
have any musical instruments, so Miss Pitts held her music
classes in the church until the new building was opened.

About 1903, while the Reverend C. W. Salter was pastor, the Boiling Springs Baptist Church had erected a new
and larger church house. However, the wooden church
building, which had been erected about 1869 and which
stood a few feet in front of the present John R. Dover
Memorial Library, was left standing. This building the
new school used as a dining hall and kitchen, a partition
separating the two rooms. Temporary tables and benches
were put in the dining room. Some of the food had to be
served cold because, with the small stove used in the kitch-
en, it was impossible to keep all the food warm. In these
cramped quarters, the first dietitian, Miss Rosa Kirby, and
the first cook, Sara Green, worked, overcoming as best
they could the many inconveniences. In addition to those
mentioned above, the water supply was not always adequate. The hydraulic ram in the spring—which students
Charles Toms, M. I. Petty, C. B. Wilson, and Oscar Duncan helped install—would cease to function at times, ne-
cessitating a bucket brigade of boys to the spring a hundred
yards away.

The first and second stories of the School Building—as
it was called then and for some years thereafter—were not
completely finished even by January 1, 1908, but suffi-
ciently so for occupancy, although, according to the first
catalogue, "the teachers and students worked under very
great disadvantage throughout the term." In the basement
were a large kitchen, a storage room, a butler's closet, and
a dining room. The first floor contained the classrooms,
auditorium, Principals' offices, and two parlors. The north
and east wings of the second floor were occupied by girls,

and the south and west wings by boys. A solid partition in the long hall on the second floor provided an invulnerable line of demarcation. Professor Huggins' quarters also were not ready when the transfer was made to the new building, and he and his family occupied a very small room on the west wing, where, in addition to the usual bedroom furniture, a large office desk, which of necessity had to be put in, added to the crampedness of the already close quarters.

One Friday evening in January, 1908—shortly after moving into the new building—two literary societies for boys were organized. J. Y. Hamrick, the Reverend Baylus Cade, the school's Financial Agent, and Professor Huggins—three men who had had experience in literary society work in the colleges which they had attended—helped the boys in the organization and in the writing of the societies' constitutions and by-laws. From time to time, they met with the boys, helping them plan programs and instructing them in public speaking and in parliamentary procedure. A committee—of which T. N. Farris and T. C. Holland were two members—was appointed to select a name for one of the societies. They chose the name Athenean, and the society elected C. B. Wilson its first president. The Reverend Baylus Cade selected the name Kalagathian for the other society, and it elected Oscar Duncan its first president.

On the same evening, following the organization of the literary societies, the Y. M. C. A. was organized, and C. B. Wilson was elected president.

The girls naturally and quite characteristically did not want to be left out, and they would not be. One night in February, a short time after the boys' societies were organized, the girls met in a large bedroom on the north wing of the School Building. Since there were only two chairs in the room, most of the girls had to sit on the floor. Mrs. Bessie Atkins Huggins, wife of the Principal, assisted the girls in organizing their society. Leila Moore was chosen president; and Maud Gold, program chairman. But what about a name for the society? A committee was appointed for that purpose—to choose a name; and the name Minnie Ramseur was chosen. At that time, Mrs. Minnie Ramseur was the largest contributor—among the women—to the school. She had given $500, no small amount in those days.

Also emulating the boys, the girls on the same evening, following the organization of their literary society, organized the Y. W. C. A. and elected Verna Humphries its president.

Another girls' society was organized in the fall of 1908. By that time, the enrollment had increased such that some of the faculty members felt that the girls should have another society. Miss Alma Smith, who taught English, Latin, and assisted in history, along with some of the charter members of the Minnie Ramseur Society, organized the new society, of which Ollie Moore was elected president. There was not another Mrs. Ramseur. So the committee selected to choose a name turned again to the Reverend Baylus Cade, and it was he who suggested Kaliergeonian.

The girls met on Friday afternoons; the boys held their meetings every Friday evening. Naturally, soon the matter of having halls in which to meet began to loom large in the minds of both the boys and the girls. Only two large rooms were available—a front room on the south corner of the School Building and a similar one on the north corner. These then were to become the society halls. The Kalagathians invited the Kaliergeonians to become their "Sister Society," and the Atheneans invited the Minnie Ramseur Society to be theirs. In their youthful enthusiasm, they set about securing the necessary funds to furnish the halls. There followed oyster suppers, ice cream suppers, and box suppers. Contributions were solicited, and even extra money that the students earned during vacations went toward the equipment. The furnishings for the society halls were bought piece by piece. However, within a few years, the halls had handsome presidents' chairs, secretaries' desks and chairs, speakers' stands, chandeliers, carpets, venetian blinds, pianos, and a number of comfortable chairs. Later a former student who had attended a senior college and who had visited other senior colleges visited again his old society hall and commented, "This hall is a credit to any society hall I have visited."

The students worked hard at their programs. A blackboard just outside each society hall door contained, a week in advance, announcements about the coming programs, which featured debates, the reading of essays, orations, and music. When assigned a part on the program, a member was expected to be responsible for it, else he would be fined. The officers served for four and one-half months rather than for the full school term, thus allowing a larger number of students to receive the training and experience coming to one who served his society in some official capacity. The constitutions and the by-laws were strictly adhered to; violations brought with them fines. A fine of twenty-five cents was assessed against a member who failed to address the president. Crossing of the legs, chewing gum, smoking, and even being slouchily dressed brought down fines on the offenders. D. C. Cole, who graduated in 1914, later said, "I belonged to the Kalagathian Literary Society, which functioned like the House of Lords. Their parliamentary procedure was perfect. . . . I have observed the United States Senate in session and it did not afford any better dignity than the old Kalagathian Literary Society."

Faculty members were welcome at the society meetings—as were visitors. Perhaps J. Y. Hamrick was one of the most frequent visitors. The school was a little more than a mile from his home; but even in the wintry weather, he would walk the distance to attend the boys' meetings. But Mr. Hamrick, who was very influential in getting the school located in Boiling Springs, was not only interested in the societies, but he was also interested in all that concerned the school and in the various activities of the school until his death in March of 1917.

In order to encourage interest in debating and oratory, the Athenean Literary Society awarded a medal to one of its members making the most improvement in debate and one to the best debater. T. C. Holland won the first Athenean best debater's medal. The Kalagathian Society awarded two similar medals. Oscar Duncan won the first Kalagathian debater's medal. In addition, the Atheneans and Kalagathians gave jointly a medal to the best orator in the two societies. These medals were coveted awards and competition for them was keen.

Much of the social life on the campus centered in the societies. In the early years of the school, the Kalagathian public debate was held in November, usually with virtually the entire student body present. At Thanksgiving, the Ramseurs and Kaliergeonians gave a joint reception for the Atheneans and Kalagathians. In early December, the Kalagathians and Kaliergeonians held their annual celebration. The Athenean public debate came the last of January. In February, the Athenean and Ramseur annual celebration took place, and the campus swarmed with former members of the societies, patrons of the school, and visitors. A happy relationship existed between town and gown; and when there was a public debate, a readers' contest, or a music recital, the auditorium would be filled with enthusiastic and interested people. Every tree on the campus became a "hitching post."

Receptions, too, were society sponsored. In March the Kaliergeonians would give a reception for the Ramseurs. The next year the situation would be reversed, with the Ramseurs putting on the reception. In April the Atheneans and Kalagathians would give a joint reception for the Ramseurs and Kaliergeonians.

Life on the campus in this "quiet country place" was by no means dull. Miss Etta Curtis, Lady Principal by 1909, usually planned a party, for instance, for all students and faculty on the night following Washington's birthday. There would usually be one couple dressed as Martha and

George, who assisted in entertaining the group. At one of these parties, Miss Curtis asked as many as could to write the first seven words of the Declaration of Independence on a slip of paper. Out of nearly two hundred, only one boy quoted the first seven words correctly. The faculty, it should be pointed out, were not asked to take part in this contest—and, no doubt, fortunately so.

Then too there were ice cream suppers, oyster suppers, and box suppers given to make money for some school project. At these suppers "the rules would be off," and the girls could go to the dining room and eat with their "special dates." This was quite a concession! For the first annual catalogue of the school plainly stated that

> It is not deemed best to neglect the culture of the social side of a student's life; therefore at suitable times there will be social gatherings in the school building under the supervision of the faculty, to which the students may invite their friends. But all invitations must be approved by the principal. On no occasion, except on holidays, will the boys and girls be allowed to associate and the girls at all times, even on holidays, must be adjacent to and under the direction of the superintendent and lady principal.

Even with the "rules off," there was perhaps a principal or superintendent ominously near, too "adjacent" for comfort or the holding of hands. But the exchange of meaningful glances, then as now, could not be prevented.

The music recitals and debates were followed by a short "social hour." Again "the rules were off," but a girl could talk to one boy for only a few minutes, and then she must move on to another. Miss Curtis liked tableaux, and her presentations were very effective. The literary societies gave very creditable plays at which there were usually no empty seats. On one occasion, a play by request was given twice. The two performances netted a total of $300. Vance Havner, later to become an outstanding North Carolina Baptist minister, was the hero of this outstanding box office success.

All, however, was not rosy during those first years of the new school. Or, on second thought, perhaps the situation may have been much rosier than anyone wished it to be. An epidemic of measles broke out the first year and swept through the student body. During the second year, everybody in school—including the teachers—had itch. Sulfur and lard were in great demand—so much so actually that the sulfur supply of the community could not meet the growing demand, and the sufferers were forced to resort to the use of axle grease as a poor substitute for the famous sulfur and lard preparation.

The course of study set up the first year of the school's operation remained substantially the same as long as the school was a high school. To be sure, some changes were made; courses were altered and added; but the departments of instruction and the courses of study remained through the years basically the same. The regular course of study covered a six-year period. This was divided into an intermediate course of two years and a high school course, further divided into A.B. and B.S. college preparatory courses of four years each. In addition, there was an English-Scientific course of three years. The A.B. college preparatory course, according to the first school catalogue, included both Latin and Greek, while the B.S. preparatory course required Latin and German. The English-Scientific course was intended for those who did not plan to go on to college. It met the needs, so it was claimed, of those preparing to teach in the public schools. There were, in addition, "a most excellent School of Music," a Commercial Department, and "a good Primary School run for the benefit of the community."

The first catalogue, which contained announcements for 1908-1909, outlined the *raison d'etre* for the various courses. Mathematics was designed to be both "disciplinary and practical" with special stress being "laid upon the principles and operations that are of constant application in the study of higher branches of mathematics and science." A first-year high school student in the college preparatory courses took higher arithmetic and algebra, plane geometry and advanced algebra his second year, solid geometry, trigonometry and surveying his third year, and analytic geometry his fourth. The work in English was "designed to give the pupils a thorough knowledge of his mother tongue, to enable him to speak and write it correctly and to acquaint him with the productions of the best writers and to instill a love for literature." History was to show the students "the development of the great plan of the ages in which individuals and nations were actors." "Accuracy in quantity and accent" was insisted upon in Greek, and students were "required constantly to translate English into Greek" and give "literal readings of the texts," which in the senior year consisted of selections from Lysaias, Isocrates, Demosthenes, and two books of the *Iliad*. Latin students wrestled with Cicero, Virgil, Livy, and Horace's satires and epistles. Physics was offered in the second year and chemistry in the third and fourth. Bible— a three-year systematic course—enabled "the student to acquire a knowledge of the Bible in its history, prophecies and precepts."

Miss Mary Clarke Pitts was the first director of the Music Department, which offered, so it was claimed, "exceptional advantages to students for pursuing their studies in Piano, Voice, and Theory." The music course was arranged for four years, but the time required to complete the course depended "to a large degree upon the ability and energy of the pupils." The work of the Intermediate Department covered two years and was in charge of the high school teachers. Intermediate students were subject to the same regulations as those of the high school, except that they were not required to join the literary societies. One room, with Miss Annie Hamrick in charge, was set apart, according to the first catalogue, for the exclusive use of the Primary Department. A reading room also was provided where the students could find "eight or ten of the best magazines, . . . daily and weekly newspapers, the *Congressional Record*, Smithsonian reports, a good dictionary and other books." Thirty cents was collected from each student annually to cover the expenses of this room.

The school sought to give its students "a thorough preparation for college and for the practical duties of life." However, "the formation of character, the cultivation of sound principles and right ideas regarding what is worth attaining in life" were esteemed of first importance. The catalogue claimed that in Boiling Springs High School intellectual development was a serious business and that students were taught to regard this as a matter upon which their best energies could well be centered. However, they were also taught that every effort should "be put forth to cultivate a character broad in its interests and forceful in its activities."

Although it would be two years yet before any students would be graduated, a full-fledged commencement program began on Sunday, May 10, 1908, and lasted until Thursday. The engraved programs announced the various events: the Sermon was to be preached Sunday evening by the Reverend J. L. Vipperman of Dallas, N. C.; the Reading Contest was to come on Monday, the Debaters' Contest on Tuesday, and the Musical Concert on Wednesday; and the Literary Address was to be delivered by Dr. Lee David Lodge, President of Limestone College, on Thursday morning. C. T. Toms was Chief Marshal; W. W. Jackson and O. N. Lovelace were Marshals from the Athenean Society, B. T. Moore and M. Q. Petty from the Kalagathian, and Miss Ollie B. Moore and Miss Maud C. Gold from the Minnie Ramseur. Miss Annie Hamrick, Paul Hamrick, and T. N. Farris served on the Entertainment Committee.

Board for many years was provided for the students on the club plan. The first catalogue estimated the board at a little over $5.50 per month. The next catalogue estimated the cost at $6.00 a month. A year or two later the estimate ranged as high as $6.50 a month. Each boarder then was required to deposit $6.50 on entrance. At the end of each school month, he was required to pay his pro-

portionate share. The $6.50 deposited at the beginning of
the term was used in payment for his board of the last
month, and any remaining part was refunded to the pupil.
During the school year 1914-1915 the board averaged
$6.34 per month; but three years later it was estimated at
from $8.00 to $8.50, and a year later it had jumped to an
estimated $9.00 to $10.50 per month.

Oscar Duncan — who entered Boiling Springs High
School as a student in the middle of the first year, 1907-
1908—was the first meat buyer for the school. He was
paid one cent a pound on foot for every cow, calf, or hog
that he bought. The meat buyer was also the butcher.
The animals were slaughtered in the woods near where
Decker Hall now stands. The butcher and the Principal
sensed the need for some kind of refrigeration. They enclosed a small room under the office of the School Building
with brick. Shelves were put in; the meat was placed on
the shelves; and blocks of ice were laid on the meat. A tin
bottom was built underneath the shelves to catch the water
from the melting ice, and the water was carried out
through a pipe. The place, however, was too damp; and
the well-planned scheme of the butcher and the Principal
came to naught.

Room rent was always kept low, probably never top-
ping the seventy-five cents to $1.00 per month of the
post-World War I years until after the school became a
junior college. In addition, however, the students had to
pay for the wood they burned in their rooms. In 1910 a
girl could get wood cut in the proper lengths and placed
in the dormitory for $3.75 for the entire year or for sev-
enty-five cents per month for the winter months beginning with November 1. The same charges were made for
wood for the boys, but the wood was not placed in the
dormitories. The rooms were equipped with all the necessary furniture, but the students were to furnish towels,
soap, lamps, oil, sheets, blankets, combs, brushes, and pil-
lows.

In 1908-1909, a first-year high school student could

attend Boiling Springs High School for $76.05 for a nine-months' term. His tuition was $18.00; his board was $49.80; other charges came to $8.25. Second-, third-, and fourth-year high school students were charged more, as were music and commercial students. Tuition charges, however, were increased later. In 1910-1911, tuition ranged from $2.00 to $3.00 per month, with the commercial students paying $18.00 for a term of eighteen weeks. Two years later the tuition charges in the High School Department had advanced another fifty cents a month.

From the first year the school had an Athletic Association. This was a student organization for the encouragement of athletics and was under the general advisory control of the faculty, but was actually supervised by the Y. M. C. A. J. G. Crawford was manager of the baseball club that first year. Bill Willis was catcher, and Howard Smith was pitcher. The baseball field, a make-shift affair with the weeds knocked down, was located where the Huggins' home now stands. At least two games were played in the spring of 1908—one with Cliffside, which Boiling Springs won 3 to 2, and one with Shelby, which was also won by Boiling Springs. This second game was played back of the grade school building. All "proper games" and sports were encouraged, the school authorities "believing them to be conducive to the best interest of the students, giving healthful mental diversion and physical exercise." However, no student was supposed to take part in any athletic contest whose grade was below 75. It was not until the school year 1913-1914 that boys' athletics were taken out of student hands and placed under the control of a faculty member, Professor Roy A. Marsh.

The School Building was completed in the early summer of 1908. Originally, as the Board had informed the Kings Mountain Association at its 1907 meeting, the building was to have cost $10,000; but because of unexpected increases in the cost of materials and labor, the cost of the building actually totaled $24,532.73, with $1,612.95 addi-

tional being spent for furniture and equipment. The Board
also spent $161.24 on certain necessary additions and im-
provements to the old church building in order to provide
living quarters for twenty boys. The grand total of all
outlays on September 24, 1908, was $25,306.92, including
$10,000 borrowed by members of the Board on their per-
sonal notes. Total collections, from all sources, amounted
to $7,866.50, while unpaid subscriptions, a part of which
were in the form of notes, amounted to $9,001.30. The
new school, after its first year of operation, found itself
$17,323.24 in debt.

A year before, in October of 1907, the Reverend Baylus
Cade had become the school's Financial Agent. On November 9, he began his work and continued until July 9,
1908, "when it was thought best to suspend the canvass
for two months, owing to the stringency in money matters." After the brief interim, he resumed his work; and
by the time the Kings Mountain Association met in 1908,
he had secured $7,392 in notes and subscriptions, but had
actually collected only $235 in cash because of the finan-
cial depression of 1907.

Professor Huggins was unanimously elected by the
Board as Principal of the school for its second year, "with
the privilege of selecting his own assistants." The original
faculty of five was now increased to nine: Mrs. Bessie
Atkins Huggins replaced Miss Lula McGee as Lady Principal; Miss Myrtle Louise Dodson was added to the music
faculty to assist Miss Pitts; other additions were F. A.
Brown, Miss Mildred McLain, the Reverend Baylus Cade,
and T. N. Farris.

The second year of Boiling Springs High School closed
on May 18, 1909, with an enrollment for the year of 219,
an increase of 84 over the first year. At the beginning of
the second year, the boys were moved out of the main
building and placed mainly in private homes in the community, the dormitory part of the main building then
being reserved exclusively for the girls and the faculty.
The Board of Trustees, however, felt that the boys should

have rooming facilities on the school grounds; but because of the already heavy debt on the school, the Board felt that it could not afford to allow the school to incur further debt. The 1909 Report of the Board of Trustees to the Kings Mountain Association, however, mentioned again a resolution passed in 1908 in which it proposed "to grant the privilege to outside parties to erect building on the school grounds to rent to students, members of the faculty, or to families desiring to patronize the school, said parties to retain title to such buildings and to collect such rental for same, . . ., till such time as this Board shall be in a position to buy said buildings." The Association was told that a friend of the school under this agreement was planning to erect three cottages on the school grounds and that one of the buildings was already under construction. The Association was further informed that "other friends of the school are now negotiating with a view of erecting a large brick building for dormitory purposes." By the time the Association met in 1910, this building—a three-story brick building with twenty-four rooms—was completed. This building, later known as "The Barn," the Board also planned to buy as soon as it was able.

At its annual meeting in May, 1909, the Board of Trustees made Professor Huggins and F. A. Brown, teacher of mathematics and science, joint Principals for a term of two years. The Board did not feel it could assume the financial responsibility for the teaching force. The Principals agreed to assume this responsibility and employed the teachers, but with the approval of the Board. Such an arrangement was destined to be short-lived. Accordingly, in the summer of 1910, the joint Principals resigned, and the Board decided "that the purposes and ends aimed at in establishing the school could best be subserved by the Board's taking over or assuming the entire management of the school." The Board was reluctant to take such a step, but the members of the Board expressed their "faith in the purpose of the churches" to stand by them. The Reverend J. M. Hamrick, a member of the 1905 Board of Trustees, was elected Principal for the 1910-1911 school year. Professor Huggins did, however, agree to serve as Assistant Principal, an arrangement which the Board felt itself fortunate in securing.

The members of the Board also felt themselves fortunate in being able to retain Miss Etta Curtis as Lady Principal—"a lady of refined culture, kind and sympathetic, rich in experience, firm and steadfast in purpose and prizing the cardinal virtues above everything else." The Board felt it could "safely assure the parents that their girls are safe when under her care." If the oil lamps were not blown out exactly at ten o'clock, Miss Curtis would go down the halls, calling out, "Blow out your lights, girls." The girls were not to talk to the boys when passing them on the campus, although it would have been as easy to have silenced Midas' wife as to have prevented such tete-a-tetes. There was to be no visiting among the girls during study hours, even though it was sometimes done. One night Miss Curtis went to visit a sick girl. The girl who had slipped in for a visit heard Miss Curtis coming and crawled under the bed. The next day she was heard to exclaim, "I thought Miss Curtis never would leave that room." Cooking, too, was forbidden in the girls' rooms, but the unmistakable aroma of cooking food or bubbling candy at times escaped from the four walls of the girls' rooms and led the ever watchful Lady Principal to the culprits. They were punished by having to copy chapters from the Bible or selections from famous orations or essays. There was an absolute rule against the passing of notes between the boys and girls. One boy is reported to have said, "I didn't write any, but I guess I passed a bushel of them." This fellow's girlfriend lived in town.

Henrietta Lucinda Curtis, the daughter of Dr. Henry and Sara Cochran Curtis and the granddaughter of Dr. Thomas Curtis, founder and first President of Limestone College in Gaffney, S. C., was born on the fourth day of September, 1858, in Catawba County, North Carolina. Miss Curtis attended Mitchell College in Statesville, N. C., and in 1874 began teaching in Hickory, N. C. She later taught in Shelby, at Fallston, N. C., which was named for her brother-in-law, Dr. B. F. Falls, at Catawba College at Newton, N. C., and at Piedmont High School, Lawndale, N. C., before coming to Boiling Springs High School. A tireless worker, she was not only on duty at all times, for girls had to be watched; but when only one eye had to be kept on them, she planted flowers and shade trees and encouraged the students to set out shrubbery and to landscape the campus. She worked tirelessly to decorate and furnish the parlors and social halls, all the while serving as Alumni Secretary. She was devoted to the school as few people ever have been, serving Boiling Springs High School and Boiling Springs Junior College for twenty-seven years. In 1936, at the age of seventy-eight, she retired. A year later, the Memorial Building burned, and she wrote a check for all her savings to help in its rebuilding. On the twenty-sixth of January, 1940, she died a pauper by choice, having given her life and her savings to the institution.

In the spring of 1910, Boiling Springs High School awarded diplomas to Miss Louise Atkins, Miss Ollie Moore, Miss Leila Moore, T. N. Farris, and T. C. Holland—its first graduating class. In addition to these, T. L. Wilson received a certificate from the Commercial Department. The Reverend C. W. Payseur preached the baccalaureate sermon on the topic "An Incomplete Building," based on I Corinthians 3:10. Miss Louise Atkins was awarded the first essay medal given by W. R. Carroll, a merchant of York, S. C. The Wake Forest Scholarship was won by T. N. Farris; but since he was not a member of the Baptist church, he felt that he should not accept it. He offered it to T. C. Holland, who had the second highest scholastic average in the graduating class. The 1910 baccalaureate address was delivered by Dr. J. B. Carlyle, Head of the Latin Department of Wake Forest College.

The Reverend J. M. Hamrick resigned the principalship at the end of the 1910-1911 school year. Professor William

J. Francis, a native of Haywood County, N. C., and a
graduate with honors from Wake Forest College, was
elected Principal. Professor Huggins continued to hold
the position of Assistant Principal.

The school completed its fourth year of operation on
May 13, 1911, with a commencement program described
as one "which would have done credit to many of our
higher institutions." Five students were graduated, three
young men and two young ladies—M. A. Stroup, O. N.
Lovelace, O. P. Hamrick, Miss Betty Lee Cade, and Mrs.
C. T. Hamrick (the last named graduated in music only).
The total enrollment was 268, an increase of 96 over the
previous year. The experiment tried by the Board of Trustees—that of assuming the full financial control of the
school—was found to be to the best interest of the school
and was to be continued. The Civic League of the school
had done much toward beautifying the campus. Water
was conveyed from a large spring by means of a hydraulic
ram to a large tank near the main building, but shortly a
movement was to get under way in the community to sink
a deep well to secure water for the school and the church.
The ram was sold when the well was dug, and the money
received was used to purchase a gasoline engine to pump
the water from the well. Chemical analysis of the water
indicated that the water, so it was reported, was "as nearly
perfect as it is possible for water to be."

The school continued to prosper under Professor Francis'
administration. The school opened in 1911 on August 15,
two weeks earlier than usual. Only one week was to be
allowed for Christmas holidays this year in order that the
school could close three weeks earlier than usual in the
spring—that is, around April 25—so that the students
from the farms might get back home and help with the
crops. The graduating class—composed of J. B. Jones,
J. P. Carlton, J. O. Ware, T. F. Harris, A. V. Hamrick,
W. T. Tate, T. L. Wilson, Miss Kate Moore, Miss Frette
Huskey, and Miss Lucy Lattimore—was double the size of
either of the two previous graduating classes, although the

total enrollment of the school dropped to 229. The deep well was sunk, insuring "the best of water near the building" and without expense to the school. Miss Curtis and the Civic League constructed some concrete walks on the campus and enclosed the yard in front of the main building with an iron railing; and the Moore Cottage, near the new Boys' Building, was remodeled as a home for the Principal.

A Department of Art, with Miss Bessie Rogers as instructor, was added to the curriculum in 1911-1912. "No education," the catalogue for 1912-1913 maintained, "is complete, in a liberal sense, which does not include a practical knowledge of drawing and an acquaintance with the principles and history of art." "A large and well adapted studio" was set up on the first floor of the main building and was supplied "with models, easels, and such material as is necessary for art work." The course was designed "to develop originality and [to] encourage the individuality of the student" in object drawing in charcoal, lead, pencil, crayon, and pen and ink; in still-life and fruits, flowers, and foliage in oils, watercolors, and pastels; in tapestry painting; in landscape painting in all the mediums; and in studies from life. The art course was a three-year one, being topped off in the senior year with a thorough course in art history, which included the history of architecture and sculpture as well as that of painting.

Professor Huggins, along with several students and "loyal friends of the school," succeeded in getting an acetylene plant installed. The actual contract price of the plant was $1,180.37; but Professor Huggins, who was agent for the company from which the plant was purchased, gave the school more than his commission. The generator was a 300-light capacity one and was enclosed in a small house at the rear of the main building. The generator, so it was claimed, was "large enough to supply the requirements of the institution should other buildings in the future be erected." By contrast with the lamps, this system of lighting was looked upon as being "almost ideal,

the light being pleasant to the eye and the cost of maintenance and the possibility of accident being reduced to
a minimum."

The Board of Trustees reported to the Kings Mountain
Association and to the Sandy Run Association in 1913 that
"under the able management of Professor W. J. Francis
and his able corps of assistants your school has made grati-
fying progress along all lines. . . . Considering the quality
of work done, [and] the ability of the teaching force to
give instruction, . . ., your Board asserts without fear of
contradiction that this school stands without a peer in this
field." Even the students were without peers. They were
virtually paragons of all students ought to be, or at least
that is the way Professor Francis described them. The
Board was told "that the order and deportment of the student body this year [1913] surpasses that of all previous
years and is as nearly perfect as human agencies can make
it. Likewise, the entire student body are interested in their
work, both in the classrooms and literary societies. The
high moral atmosphere which has characterized the school
in the past is again manifest this year in increased propor-
tions." The Board also commended Miss Rosa Kirby, "a
graduate in Domestic Science" and one who knew "how
to practice economy with the maximum of efficiency."
"Not a single complaint against board has ever reached
this Board," it was reported, "either from student or
patron, during the entire time Miss Kirby has been our
Matron." *Tempora mutantur, nos et mutamur in illis.*

Perhaps not all the credit ought to go to Miss Kirby.
The school had been fortunate in having, through the
years, some loyal and self-sacrificing cooks. Sara Green,
the school's first cook, served only one year, but the hard-
ships were perhaps greater that year than they have ever
been since. Texana Green was a cook for two years, Bertha
Wray for ten years, Essie Roberts for nine years, and Ger-
trude Jeffries for twenty years, which includes the time
she was head cook for the College. Along with these, there
were Annie Watkins, Aunt Missie Thompson, Rosetta

Wray, and Macie Green, who helped in the kitchen. At first no recommendations were required of the cooks, but on one occasion one came to talk with the Principal about working in the kitchen. Without his even asking for it, she gave the following recommendation: "I am all alone and by myself; I am single and not married, and I have no children; and I would rither cook." She got the job. Ulus Hamilton served in several capacities in the school over a period of years. He cooked, washed dishes, cleaned the dining room, helped at every banquet, and was butler when teas and receptions were held.

Professor Francis resigned the principalship in April of 1914, and a few months later Professor J. D. Huggins again became Principal of Boiling Springs High School. The progress which characterized the administration of Professor Francis continued; improvements abounded. In the early fall of 1914, the school had an enrollment of 209, "the largest in its history at this season, there being 122 boys and 87 girls. These represent fifteen counties in the two Carolinas and Georgia." Twenty-five were enrolled in the Primary Department and fifty-three in the Preparatory Department; there were sixty-eight high school freshmen, twenty-one sophomores, twenty juniors, and seventeen seniors; twenty-three were enrolled in the Music Department, six in the Art Department, and forty-six in the Bible Department. The literary societies equipped each of the society halls with pianos, and the Athenean and Ramseur Societies painted the interior of the auditorium. Flower gardens were planted near the main building, and the students took pride in caring for the grassy lawns on the campus. Through the efforts of Miss Etta Curtis and others, "a complete system of water works with a 1500-gallon iron compressed-air tank and with a large concrete septic tank more than 300 feet from the rear of the building" was installed. Funds were collected from here, there, and yon to pay for the $1,045.91 improvement; and by the fall of 1915, only $300.00 remained to be raised. A

year later Miss Curtis lacked only $50.00. In the fall of
1915, another badly needed improvement was nearing
completion: the Gaston Plumbing and Heating Company
was installing a steam heating plant for the main building.
The $2,224.00, which the project cost, was furnished by
E. B. Hamrick, Dr. J. W. Wood, S. B. Turner, Wiley
Hamrick, Carme Elam, O. P. Hamrick, and George P.
Glenn. These men were to hold the title to the heating
plant until the Board could buy the plant "at actual first
cost." The Board proposed to collect rental for the heat
furnished and to pay the investors an annual dividend of
8 per cent. A separate, but similar, heating plant was also
provided for the Boys' Dormitory and the Moore Cottage
at a cost of $775.00, the money being furnished by E. B.
Hamrick, Wiley Hamrick, O. P. Hamrick, and George P.
Glenn under conditions similar to those agreed upon earlier
for the first heating plant.

As if to dramatize the need for central heating, a trag-
edy—the worst in the history of the school—occurred in
the winter of 1915. Wood-burning stoves were then still
being used in the Boys' Dormitory. The students were
getting ready to leave for the Christmas holidays. W. G.
Zimmerman set about to light one of the old wood-burn-
ers: he poured just a little kerosene from a gallon kerosene
can on some green wood; he then struck a match; but his
fire would not burn. He poured on some more kerosene
and struck some more matches until—perhaps no one
knows just how—the kerosene became ignited, and there
was an explosion. Zimmerman was alone at the time; all
other boys had gone to breakfast. The sound of the explo-
soin sent the boys scurrying back to the dormitory. They
heard Zimmerman screaming. The door to his room, however, was locked; but the boys knocked out a panel of the
door and unlocked it. When they reached him, the cloth-
ing on his body was still aflame. He was rushed to the
Rutherford Hospital, but died three days later.

An expanding curriculum brought with it the need for

additional recitation rooms, which were not to be had in the already crowded main building. When the Department of Domestic Science—later called the Department of Household Arts—and the Department of Art and China Painting were added to the curriculum in 1916, the administration, as if to indicate that history had come full cycle, turned again to the old church building and this time converted it into three classrooms at a total cost of approximately $175.00, with another $150.00 being spent to furnish the rooms for the Primary Department, the Art Department, and the Domestic Science Department. The new department—Domestic Science—aimed, so the catalogue claimed, at giving "young women the scientific and practical instruction that will enable them to become efficient housekeepers and home-makers," or at giving them "a thorough knowledge of the technical subjects and related sciences that will enable them to become matrons and housekeepers in public or private institutions."

In the fall of 1915 Professor Huggins informed the Board of Trustees that the "school is, at present, in splendid condition. The health of the student body is extremely good. Never before has the student body, as a whole, shown a greater tendency to respect the regulations and to apply themselves better to their studies." Naturally, just at this time, Professor Huggins would have been concerned about health, but with him the health of others, since his own health was then so precarious; but quite characteristically, he said nothing about his own health, so far as we know. Early in the 1915 summer vacation, Professor Huggins became critically ill from a resurgence of the trouble he had had in his youth. He was hospitalized, and his right leg was amputated above the knee. He could not that summer do his usual public relations work and student procurement, but by fall he was back at his desk, looking after the affairs of the school.

Friends of the school, students, townsfolk, yea even the Trustees were delighted at the school's progress through

the years, although for the Trustees the debt, which hung
like a dark and ominous cloud over an otherwise bright
situation, kept them in the slough of reality and prevented
any enduring jubilation on their part. It was ten years
from the time the students first moved into the main building before the debt on the building was liquidated. In
1909 the balance on the indebtedness was $15,675.00, hav-
ing been reduced by only $1,648.24 from the year before;
but if interest and insurance were added to the balance,
the total indebtedness then aggregated $16,951.00. At their
1908 meetings, the two Associations had appointed committees to work out an equitable division of the indebtedness between the Associations. On the basis of membership, $9,885.15 with interest was apportioned to the Kings
Mountain Association and $5,491.75 with interest to the
Sandy Run Association. In making the apportionment,
$2,215.00 was deducted from the total indebtedness since
unpaid subscriptions in the Boiling Springs community
would take care of that amount. The indebtedness was
further apportioned among the various churches of the
Associations. Between the fall of 1909 and the fall of 1910,
$2,076.00 was paid on the indebtedness, leaving approxi-
mately $14,875.00. The greater part of this indebtedness
was in the form of joint notes signed by members of the
Board of Trustees; thus there was in actuality little or no
encumbrance on the school property, at that time valued
at approximately $30,000.

By the next meeting of the Kings Mountain Association
at Elizabeth Church on September 21-23, 1911, no substantial reduction had been made in the indebtedness.
Money was slow in coming in. "Your Board is suffering
under this burden," the Trustees' Report stated, "but your
School is suffering more!" About $4,000 had already been
paid in interest alone. "How much longer shall this sui-
cidal procedure continue?" the Board asked. The entire
$810 collected since the report the year before had been
applied to interest; and as if to underscore the seriousness
of the situation, it was further reported that only two

churches—Zoar and Sandy Plains—had paid their apportionment with interest, and only four—Shelby, Zion, Mt. Pleasant, and Green River—had paid their apportionment minus the interest.

However, at Mt. Zion the next year the complexion of things had changed somewhat: $2,300.00 had been paid during the Associational year on the principal; but, alas, $1,346.00 had gone for interest. Five churches—Zoar, Sandy Plains, Lattimore, Elizabeth, and Mt. Zion—had paid their distributive share with interest and ten—Shelby, Zion, Mt. Pleasant, Green River, Caroleen, Henrietta, High Shoals, Bethlehem, Pleasant Hill, and Ross Grove—had paid their distributive share without interest. At the 1912 Associatonal meetings a resolution by George L. English was adopted by each Association authorizing the appointment of an Advisory Committee of seven from each of the two Associations to confer with the Board and to devise ways and means for the early liquidation of the indebtedness. The following were appointed from the Kings Mountain Association: George L. English, James T. Bowman, A. E. Bettis, J. W. Kendrick, D. J. Keeter, J. T. S. Mauney, and G. W. Hamrick; and from the Sandy Run Association, the following were appointed: A. M. Lovelace, M. M. Green, A. I. Jolley, the Reverend J. M. Goode, J. P. D. Withrow, J. A. Carlton, and A. L. Smart.

This Committee met at the Sandy Run Baptist Church, together with the Board, on October 17, 1912. There were, in addition, several pastors present: the Reverends Z. D. Harrill, A. C. Irvin, L. W. Swope, B. P. Greene, Baylus Cade, D. G. Washburn, J. G. Graham, J. R. Miller, B. M. Bridges, and I. D. Harrill. J. H. Quinn from the Board of Trustees was elected chairman and George L. English secretary. After an all-day session, interspersed at intervals with prayer, a plan was decided upon which "resulted in the practical liquidation of the indebtedness." At the meeting $4,250.00 was subscribed, with the subscriptions being conditioned upon the *whole* amount's being subscribed and "canvassers being put in the field." The

Committee, it was later reported, "went away buoyant
with the hope of success." The canvassers—among whom
were G. E. Lineberry, the Reverend J. W. Suttle, T. Carl
Hamrick, the Reverend J. M. Goode, and E. B.Hamrick—
got to work; and the sanguineness of the Committee
proved to be no fireflaught, for by the latter part of September, 1913, $11,685.00 had been paid on the indebted-
ness, leaving a balance of only $1,492.63. It was not, how-
ever, until January 2, 1917, that the old debt was fully
paid and the cancelled notes burned in public.

World War I came and caused some disturbance in what
could otherwise have been several halcyon years. Even
during the war years, "continual and substantial progress
along all lines" continued to be reported in enrollment, in
standards of scholarship, and in Christian influence. Many
boys of military age, of course, were called into the service; but these were more than compensated for by the
increase in the number of girls enrolled. By the fall of
1918, however, the draft age had been lowered to eighteen;
the Board of Trustees viewed this with a great deal of concern. Their only hope, so it seemed just then, lay in a plan
being worked out by the Committee on Education and
Special Training of the War Department which would
allow the organization of a training corps on the Boiling
Springs High School campus under the supervision of the
War Department similar to that provided for in the colleges. "Should this not materialize," the Board reported
in September of 1918, "then we will soon lose all boys 18
and upward." Before the plan materialized, however, the
Armistice was signed on November 11, 1918; and the
imminent threat to the school vanished and was forgotten
in the rejoicing that "it was over over there."

At the Ross Grove Church in 1920 Professor J. D. Huggins read the Report on Christian Education to the Kings
Mountain Association. It was in reality an eloquent plea
for Christian education and the support of Christian
schools through endowment. "We should . . . view Christian education in its relation to the masses of the people,"

Professor Huggins said. "For upon the right education of the people depends the life of our democratic nation, and upon the life of the nation depends the progress of the church." He continued: "Christian schools must continue to furnish a majority of the leaders of the church and state." But, as he put it, "the unvarying history of Christian schools seems to be that they are endowed or they die. We would therefore recommend that the Association take steps at the earliest practical date to systematically endow their school." But more buildings and consequent years of debt were destined to come before any substantial endowment was provided for the school.

The enrollment continued its upward surge. It was over three hundred in 1918-1919, and the need for a new building large enough to house several of the departments and to provide a larger auditorium was apparent. The academic year 1919-1920 was described as the most successful in the history of the school; the total enrollment was 366, an increase of 51 over the year before; and if the school had had adequate facilities, from 100 to 150 more students could have been enrolled. All rooms for girls were assigned before the end of the first week of school, and some private homes in the community where students had been housed formerly were no longer available. If the enrollment was to continue to increase, additional classrooms would be needed as well as a more adequate dining room. It was now not a question of more teachers or students; they could be had if there were space.

Accordingly in 1919, the Board of Trustees began what has been described as a "vigorous campaign to secure pledges and subscriptions to the amount of $40,000 to erect a new three-story building as a memorial to all soldiers and sailors who went out from this school and from the territory of the Kings Mountain and Sandy Run Associations to the World War and to their mothers." Three former students of Boiling Springs High School had been killed during the course of the War. They were Ira Crab-

tree, Norwood Huggins, and C. Meade Ewing. This building, as originally planned, was to contain an auditorium,
society halls, and classrooms for the Departments of Music,
Art, Household Arts and Science, as well as a gymnasium
and a banquet hall. The desired amount was pledged, and
the work of construction on what was to be called the
Memorial Building began in the spring of 1920. By the
fall, the work on the building was well under way. Leaders
in the building program hoped that the brick work would
be completed and a roof put on the building before the
severe winter weather came. But contracts for labor and
materials were let only up to the amount of subscriptions
in sight. The Board had promised "to create no debts on
this building beyond money in sight," and this promise it
was determined to keep "unless otherwise advised by the
Associations." The Board was hoping, however, that at
the 1920 sessions of the Associations it would be otherwise
advised. There had been what the Board characterized as
a "remarkable increase in the price of labor and materials"
since the building was planned, and now approximately
$20,000 additional was needed to complete the building.
The Board sought immediate action. "Uncompleted," it
reminded the Associations, "this building will be of no
value." But for several reasons, not the least of which was
the depression of 1921, the building was not finally completed until late in 1925.

In 1920 the North Carolina Baptist Educational Board
apportioned Boiling Springs High School $16,500 from
the Seventy-Five Million Campaign to be used as follows:
$6,000 to purchase Boys' Dormitory, Moore Cottage, and
the steam heating plants; $500 to equip a chemical labora-
tory; and $2,000 a year for five years to help meet current
operating expenses. The expense of operating the school
in 1920-1921 was $46,164.55. Of this amount, $13,435.74
went for teachers' salaries; $921.87 for equipment and re-
pairs; $600.50 as salary for the night watchmen; $3,036.45
for fuel; $624,25 for lights; $8,075.36 for incidental expenses; and $19,470.41 for the boarding department. In-

come for the year was $47,870.43. Of this amount $10,172.50 was paid in tuition by the 309 students; $19,-470.41 was paid for board; $1,197.75 for room rent; $3,036.45 for heat; $624.25 for lights; $5,651.68 for incidentals; $5,022.79 was paid to the special departments; $2,630 was received from the Baptist State Educational Board, and $64.60 was received from endowment. Of this amount, a total of $44,836.36 had been collected by the fall of 1921.

During the academic year of 1920-1921, electric lights were installed in all the buildings, replacing the outmoded acetylene lights, an improvement brought about largely through the efforts of Professor O. P. Hamrick and certain others who worked with him.

According to B. E. "Pop" Simmons, the first football game playing in Cleveland County was played at Boiling Springs in the fall of 1920. Simmons, now veteran coach at Lattimore, N. C., High School but then a student at Boiling Springs, arranged for the game. Gaffney, S. C., High School, a pioneer in football in the Piedmont Carolinas, had challenged Boiling Springs High School; and, according to Simmons, "our name was at stake." Boiling Springs High School had no football coach, but Simmons, who served as coach, had seen one game. The Boiling Springs boys practiced all week, using an old shoe for a ball. When Saturday came, "Pop" hustled his boys out on the field, dressed in four or five pairs of pants and as many shirts, the whole padded lot bedecked with a top layer of overalls. "That Gaffney crowd looked at our size with all that rig on," "Pop" later reported, "and they just folded up." The lone referee of the game was Adam Whisnant, a Boiling Springs resident who had seen a few football games while in the Navy during World War I. Clyde Jones, later an All-Southern football player at Wake Forest College, C. C. "Cobby" Horn, now a Shelby, N. C., attorney, and the Reverend Horace G. Hammett of Columbia,

S. C., were among the players on the Boiling Springs team, which won 6-0.

The Kings Mountain and Sandy Run Associations were eager that other nearby Baptist Associations join with them in supporting the Boiling Springs High School. In 1919, the young Gaston County Baptist Association appointed a special committee to visit the school. This committee made a favorable report in 1920, recommending that the Gaston Association accept the invitation to become one of the joint owners of the school. The Gaston Association was a little wary, however. It did not object to becoming a joint owner if that did not mean a three-way split of the indebtedness. It did not reject the favorable report but appointed another committee to make further investigations and to submit a further report at the 1921 session of the Association. The Gaston Association was not the only Association approached with this proposition; the South Fork Association too was asked to become a joint-sponsor with the other Associations.

The South Fork Association apparently determined to leave the school to others, but the Gaston Association joined with the Kings Mountain and Sandy Run Associations "in the ownership and control" of the Boiling Springs High School. However, the Gaston Association "would assume no financial responsibilities of the school, old or new, until the expiration of the five years covered by the Seventy-Five Million Campaign, as the churches of that Association had gone their limit for Christian education in that campaign." The Gaston Association was given ten members on the Board of Trustees, making a total of thirty-five members. These ten men, described as "men of exceptional ability and deeply interested in Christian education," were appointed to serve until the 1922 session of the Association when their successors would "be regularly named by that body in such a manner and for such length of term as it may elect." The school's charter was amended to give the Gaston Association equal rights and status with the other two. Now the school was supported by 23,000 Baptists, and the Trustees were sanguine of the future success of the school. In fact, the future success of the school, as they put it, was assured.

A bright future did not necessarily mean a bright present. In fact, the partly completed Memorial Building cast an ominous shadow over an otherwise bright present. There it stood, the hull of a building, covered over and nearly closed in but with very little work done on the interior—the work having been stopped for lack of funds. That is, the work was stopped until a gift of $1,000 by J. F. Alexander of nearby Forest City set the workmen to work again temporarily on the interior. By the fall of 1922, more than $46,000 had been spent on a building that had been of very little use to the school, and an estimated $15,728.10 was yet needed to complete the building. The Board reminded the Kings Mountain and Sandy Run Associations at their 1922 sessions of the Board's instructions not to borrow money, and borrow it would not without approval of the Associations. No borrowing, however, meant that work on the building must be discontinued. The Associations could take their choice. The Associations relented and allowed the Board to borrow some money— $2,150 was borrowed, in this case—with which the exterior of the building was completed and the auditorium nearly so. The students and teachers of Boiling Springs High School undertook to raise the nearly $2,000 necessary "to seat the Auditorium with opera chairs." Even yet between $9,000 and $10,000 would be required to complete the building.

In 1923, "after careful deliberation," as the Trustees' Report put it, but quite likely in desperation, the Board decided unanimously to float a $40,000 bond issue to be secured by a mortgage or deed of trust on the school property. The money was to be used to pay off the indebtedness on the Memorial Building, to complete the building, to install a central heating plant, to purchase the privately-owned interest in the heating plant then being used, and

to erect "an elevated water tank." On the first day of
January, 1924, the bonds, paying six per cent interest and
maturing in five series of $8,000 each, were issued. By fall,
however, only about a third or less of the bonds had been
sold. There was doubt that these were gilt-edged, blue-
chip securities; and the Board was asked, "How do you
propose meeting the principal and interest of these bonds
as they mature?" The Board replied: "These three great
Associations, with an aggregate of more than 100 churches
and more than 26,000 members, will find a way to provide
for that. They have not failed us yet; they will not fail
us in the future." But the Board actually was looking beyond the three Associations for approval and financial
backing—both of which it got from the Educational Board
of the Baptist State Convention of North Carolina. The
Educational Board approved the issuance of the bonds, and
it agreed to pay in 1925 the $2,400 interest on the bonds.

There were those, however, who wanted more—more
than the $2,400—from the Baptist State Convention of
North Carolina. On October 2, 1924, Professor Huggins
presented a resolution to the Kings Mountain Association
at its annual meeting, requesting the Association to request
the Educational Board of the Baptist State Convention to
request the Baptist State Convention of North Carolina
"at its approaching session, to assume the responsibility for
the payment of the bonded indebtedness on the Boiling
Springs High School with the distinct understanding that
said school shall make no further indebtedness without the
consent of said Educational Board to the end that these
three Associations may concentrate their entire efforts in
behalf of the Convention's financial program as a whole,
. . ." The resolution passed, and the Baptist State Convention agreed in part—agreed at least to *guarantee* the
interest and $32,000 of the principal of the bonds. But
even with this underwriting, only $13,200 of the bonds
had been sold by the fall of 1925. The bond houses, at
least most of them, shied away from such bonds, preferring
municipal bonds that were based on the power of taxation.

However, a St. Louis firm, Bitting and Company, did agree to take the entire issue on the same terms that it had purchased bonds of other North Carolina Baptist Schools.

The Memorial Building, which ultimately cost approximately $65,000, was completed in 1925. This now became the Administration Building, containing not only the Principal's office but all classrooms as well. And as a further sign of the progress and excellence of the school, it was elected to membership in the Southern Association of Colleges and Secondary Schools.

Now that the school had adequate facilities and was fully accredited regionally, a new threat arose which threatened to choke out the very life of the school. It was obvious to everyone that the school could not compete with the tax-supported State high school system, then rapidly spreading into all corners of North Carolina. In 1924-1925, there were 272 students enrolled in Boiling Springs High School; but in 1925-1926, only 224; the next year, the school had 184 students; but in 1927-1928, only 138, only three more students than it had the first year of its operation. The trend was obvious by 1926, and the Trustees squarely faced the problem and asked the Associations to do the same. The Board offered the following resolution: "Resolved that this Board recommend to the Associations that this school become a junior college the next scholastic year [1927-28]." Dr. Zeno Wall, pastor of the First Baptist Church of Shelby, in turn offered the following resolution of endorsement to the Kings Mountain Association: "Resolved that this Association endorse and approve the recommendations of the Board of Trustees of Boiling Springs High School, looking toward making it a junior college, and that a committee of five be appointed by the Association to confer with like committees from the Sandy Run and Gaston Associations, which committees shall confer with the State Board of Education of our Baptist denomination as to ways and means by which this is to be accomplished, and that this committee be given full power to act." This resolution was adopted by a rising vote, and the committee from the Kings Mountain Association, composed of J. H. Quinn, C. J. Black, Dr. Zeno Wall, E. B. Hamrick, and D. J. Keeter, was appointed.

The other two Associations followed the lead of the Kings Mountain Association, and the recommendation that Boiling Springs High School become a junior college was submitted to the Educational Board of the North Carolina Baptist State Convention. The recommendation was passed on to the new General Board of the Convention, which, in turn, authorized its General Secretary, Dr. Charles E. Maddrey, "to come to this territory and meet a delegation from this Board to see if some plan could be evolved that would protect the future of our school and promote the best interest of the Centennial Campaign now starting for the relief of our Baptist schools." Dr. Maddrey met with the Executive Committee of the Board, together with a number of pastors and friends of the school, at the First Baptist Church in Shelby on October 2, 1927. Dr. Maddrey and the members of the Board worked out a mutually satisfactory agreement, which was later to go to the Associations for their approval and also to the Baptist State Convention, which was to meet at Durham, N. C., in November, for its "acceptance, amendment, or rejection." The tentative agreement set the amount which the General Board would pay the Boiling Springs High School for the current operations for 1928 and 1929 at $3,500 per calendar year. The Trustees also agreed to cooperate with the General Board in putting "on jointly one great Centennial Campaign early in the year 1928 among the Baptists and non-Baptists in the churches and territories embraced in the Kings Mountain and Sandy Run Associations for a goal not less than $250,000 and the sum raised shall be divided as follows: (1) The debt of $40,000 carried by the Convention for Boiling Springs shall be paid and discharged; (2) The remainder shall be divided between the General Board of the State Convention and the Trustees of Boiling Springs High School by the following

ratio, *viz*: 40 per cent to the Convention and 60 per cent
to the Trustees of Boiling Springs High School." In the
meantime, the Trustees were authorized to "add one year's
work above the high school grade beginning with the session of 1928, and may be permitted to raise Boiling Springs
High School to the full standard of a junior college beginning with the session of 1929." After the $40,000 debt
was paid, one-half of the funds received by the school were
then to be used for permanent improvements, and one-half
was to go into the endowment fund.

There were some who were a little apprehensive about
the school's becoming a junior college. What if the junior
college movement proved to be just a passing fad? But
actually the school was taking little risk; for if it remained
a preparatory school, it was sure to be choked out by the
encircling public high schools. To become a junior college
seemed the only plausible way to prevent inevitable ex-
tinction. The Report on Education, read to the Kings
Mountain Association by the Reverend Rush Padgett at
its 1927 session at Double Shoals Church, attempted to
assure the delegates that junior colleges were not educational freaks but were "likely to remain . . . a distinct part
of the educational program in America." The Associations
were reminded of the great American educational ideal—
the desire to educate the masses. Consequently, it was
argued, there will be "a tendency to lower the period of
general education from eleven years in high school, plus
four years in college, to eleven or twelve years in high
school, plus two years in college." The junior college, the
Report maintained, would meet such a demand.

The last report of the Trustees to the three Associations,
while the institution was still a high school, was made by
J. H. Quinn, Chairman of the Board. He pointed to the
splendid preparation that the school had offered its students and to the splendid records made by its graduates.
For the first time in its history, he reported, the school
closed a year (1926-27) with a deficit in operating expenses. The deficit—$1,393.40—was attributed to at least

three circumstances beyond the school's control. First, there was the generally known and bemoaned decrease in enrollment; secondly, the school failed to receive an expected $2,000 from the Alexander estate; and finally, the General Board of the Baptist State Convention found it impossible to contribute as much to current operations as had been expected.

On the second day of May, 1928, Boiling Springs High School closed its twenty-first year of work and its last as a high school. This was a time of "such sweet sorrow"—a time of backward glancing—a time of reminiscing. The Associations were reminded of the strenuous years, marked by sacrificial devotion and unrelenting efforts on the part of faithful and loyal friends of the institution. The Baptists of the three sponsoring Associations could be justly proud of the school's achievements "in this section where the Baptist cause so largely predominates." The wisdom of these Associations in entering the field of Christian education was now apparent. Thousands of students had enrolled in the school; five hundred eighty-eight had graduated.

Many of those five hundred eighty-eight became ministers, physicians, lawyers, teachers, and businessmen. At least two became nationally known. Martin Dewey Whitaker, at this writing, is the highly honored President of Lehigh University of Bethlehem, Pennsylvania. Following his graduation from Wake Forest College in 1927, he did graduate study at the University of North Carolina and New York University, receiving the Ph.D. degree from New York University in 1935. Since then he has been honored with Doctor of Law degrees from Lafayette College (1946) and Rutgers University (1948) and with Doctor of Science degrees from Moravian College (1947) and Wake Forest College (1947). The other, Wilbur Joseph Cash, is famous for a book, still a best seller, which he published in 1941. His MIND OF THE SOUTH is a critical analysis of the social background, temperament, and characteristic ways of the Southerner. A reviewer in the

Atlantic Monthly, April, 1941, said, "These 400-odd brilliant pages by a Southern journalist possess the power to make understanding flourish and triumph in one of the areas where bigotry and misunderstanding have been the norm for a century. The book is a literary and moral miracle." *Current History and Forum,* June, 1941, said that "the book will have an honored place in the growing literature of the South. In fact, the candor, forthrightness, and energy of the author make it easily one of the most revealing books we have yet had on any region in America."

3

Boiling Springs Junior College—
1928-1942

O<small>N THE</small> third day of September, 1928, Boiling Springs Junior College opened for its first session. The Reverend James Blaine Davis, a graduate of Mars Hill College, Wake Forest College, the University of North Carolina, and Southwestern Baptist Theological Seminary, had been elected President. President Davis came to Boiling Springs Junior College from a pastorate at the Henderson Street Baptist Church of Cleveland, Texas. Some years earlier, in 1918-19, he had served as an instructor at North Carolina State College; and for four years, 1919-1923, he was an instructor at the University of North Carolina. On September 10, in the college auditorium, Mr. Davis was formally installed as President, at which time he made what *The Kalarathea* described as "a stirring speech . . . predicting that the Junior College would be a success and, in the years to come, [that] it would become the educational center of the Piedmont section" of North Carolina.

President Davis also addressed the Kings Mountain Association at its 1929 session. Before his address, however, he presented Professor Huggins, Dean of the College; and before the assembled delegates, "they pledged each other their loyalty and cooperation in carrying forward the work of the institution." President Davis then spoke to the Association on "Hidden Treasures in World Redemption."

At this 1928 meeting, the College faculty also were introduced to the delegates of the Association. Miss Etta Curtis had been named Dean of Women. Professors O. P. Hamrick and H. G. Hammett were teachers of English, with Professor Hammett also teaching mathematics. The modern languages were taught by Professor Henry L. Snuggs, while Mrs. J. D. Huggins taught Latin. Miss Eunice Kneece taught history and Miss Martha Reece science. Miss Lorene Woody was assistant in music. Household arts were taught by Miss Ruth McCown, and the Reverend J. L. Jenkins, pastor of the Boiling Springs Baptist Church, taught the courses in religious education. Mrs. Lillian M. Ritch continued as dietitian.

There were 78 college students and 124 academic and special students enrolled in 1928-1929. The 78 college students were all enrolled in freshman courses, the second year of college work not being added until the next academic year. There were six departments in the college—English, Mathematics, Natural Science, Foreign Language, Social Science, Bible, and Education. The same departments were also in the academic division, with the exception of Education. The three special departments were Music, Voice, and Physical Education. To receive the diploma, "Associate in Letters," a college student had to complete sixty-six semester hours of college work and, in addition, submit a thesis of not less than 2,500 words on a subject approved by the professor in whose department it was written.

A joint campaign was "launched and vigorously prosecuted during the summer [of 1928] within the Kings Mountain and Sandy Run Associations to reach a goal of $250,000 for the Centennial Fund and to make Boiling Springs High School a junior college." This was done in keeping with the agreement tentatively adopted earlier by the Board and the General Secretary of the Convention. The agreement was ratified, with a few slight amendments, by the Baptist State Convention at its meeting in November of 1927. Although a little less than half the goal was reached, the campaign in the two Associations was considered "a marked success and fully demonstrated the deep interest of our people in the movement for the College." The bonded debt of $40,000 against the institution could now be paid, if all pledges were made good. The remainder was to be "divided between the College and the Centennial Fund on the basis of 60 per cent to the former and 40 per cent to the latter." The College planned to use half of its sum for equipment, and the rest was to go into endowment.

The Associations were told in 1928 that "no efforts will be spared in making ours a standard junior college." To accomplish this goal, no efforts *could* be spared; and at times even the best efforts seemed hardly enough. It was soon discovered that the money problem was ubiquitous: income had to be provided—$5500 annually—over and above the income from tuition and incidental charges if the College was to meet standardization requirements. Consequently, at the 1929 session of the Kings Mountain Association, B. T. Falls offered a resolution, which was passed, requesting the churches "to raise funds for Boiling Springs Junior College annually, and over and above the amounts regularly contributed to the Cooperative Program of the General Board of the Baptist State Convention." The necessary additional $5,500 annually was to be equitably divided among the three cooperating Associations.

The College sought accreditation from the North Carolina State Department of Public Instruction through the North Carolina College Conference. A survey was made and a report of the survey—signed by Dr. A. T. Allen, Superintendent of Public Instruction; Dr. James E. Hillman, Director of Certification; and Dr. J. Henry Highsmith of the Division of School Inspection—was sent to the College. The report pointed out that, since the College had been in operation only one year and since the North Carolina College Conference provided for the rating of colleges on the two-year or four-year basis, it was felt that the work of the institution could not properly be evaluated at that time; and it was suggested that the "rating be deferred until plans now under consideration be carried out during the session of 1929-1930, the rating to depend upon compliance with the standards of the North Carolina College Conference." The report, however, did offer certain suggestions. The College Departments should be staffed by Heads of Departments whose training should be in keeping with the standards of the College Conference. Although the chemistry equipment was valued at $2000, the laboratory was not satisfactory; and the biology laboratory was too small and not adequately equipped. The library was inadequate; more library space was needed; standard library furniture should be installed; and a trained librarian should be secured. Not a single classroom was equipped with modern seats or desks suitable for college students. The rooms themselves needed renovating; or, as the report put it, "a liberal use of paint would improve the interior of the building" and "linoleum, or other floor covering, should be provided for the rough cement floors." The gymnasium was unfinished but "should be completed and equipped at the earliest possible date." The productive endowment of the College should be increased to at least $100,000 and the indebtedness "liquidated at the earliest possible time." And a new building, with modern class rooms and modern equipment, "should be provided, in order that standard college work can be given; the present building is unsatisfactory, from many standpoints."

The picture was a dark one. Money was needed—a lot of money. The College must be accredited, else, as one friend of the school wrote J. H. Quinn, Chairman of the Board of Trustees, "the old students may be reluctant to

return and new students will not care to come without
assurance that . . . conditions will be met and hence doubt
removed about the school [sic] being standardized."

In June of 1929, to make the picture even darker, Professor Huggins resigned from the College faculty. A year
before, he had understood Dr. Hillman of the State Department of Public Instruction to say that, if three of
the five Department Heads held M.A. degrees and if the
other teachers were actively progressing toward degrees,
then all would be well. Now, however, a year later, President Davis received a letter from the State Department of
Public Instruction indicating that Professor Huggins
should not head a department. Six weeks before, Professor
Huggins had received a letter, dated April 26, 1929, from
President Davis, officially notifying him that the Trustees
had elected him Dean and Head of the Mathematics Department at a salary of $2,200. On June 13, 1929, Pro-
fessor Huggins wrote the Board of Trustees, requesting
release for both himself and Mrs. Huggins from the positions to which they had been elected. As Professor Huggins said in another letter, he felt that, if he were to
continue to teach in the College, he would have to continue graduate work, even at the sacrifice of his health.
Another position had been offered to him and Mrs. Huggins which, he felt, would offer an opportunity for service.
But even then Professor Huggins' thoughts were of the
welfare of Boiling Springs Junior College: two teachers,
he pointed out, could perhaps be employed on his salary
of $2,200 and certainly three could be hired on his salary
plus that of Mrs. Huggins. Professor Huggins, however,
was not destined to stay long from Boiling Springs Junior
College. Within a year he was back to stay until his death
on April 19, 1932.

On the fifteenth of May, 1930, Dr. J. Henry Highsmith,
Director of the Division of School Inspection of the North
Carolina State Department of Public Instruction, wrote
Chairman Quinn of the Board of Trustees to inform him
of the action of the College Rating Board on May 12.

Boiling Springs Junior College had been given a conditional rating as a standard junior college for the session 1929-30. This action was based, it was pointed out, on Mr. Quinn's letter of the sixth of May in which he indicated the arrangement whereby the necessary income for the College was to be secured for the 1930-31 session. The College was to be inspected during the next session (1930-1931); and if satisfactory financial arrangements were made for the support of the College and *all* other requirements for a standard junior college met, the rating could "be continued without condition." As Dr. Highsmith phrased it, "the big problem ahead of Boiling Springs is, of course, the matter of adequate support." Whether or not there was any "method" in the College's "madness" is hard to say; but Dr. J. Henry Highsmith delivered the literary address at the College commencement on May 20, 1931.

President James B. Davis resigned early in 1930. The Trustees accepted his resignation, which he quested of the Board through the Board's Chairman, J. H. Quinn—the resignation to become effective on May 20, 1930. On the fifth of May, Dr. Zeno Wall, pastor of the First Baptist Church of Shelby, was elected temporary President of the College; and Professor J. D. Huggins was re-elected Dean of the College, after an interim of one year. Professor Huggins was also made Principal of the High School division. On May 7, *The Cleveland Star* carried an announcement by Mr. Quinn stating that $5,000 had been raised to insure a standard junior college. On May 21, the day after President Davis' resignation became effective, the *Star* reported that Dr. Wall had accepted the presidency of Boiling Springs Junior College—a position he occupied without pay.

Along came the Great Depression, but in spite of it the College opened for its 1930-31 session on September 2 with the largest enrollment in the College's history—97 in the College and 106 in the High School division. The three

Associations were told in the fall of 1930 that the College had "met all the standard requirements as to physical equipment and faculty qualifications," and that every Department was "headed by a teacher holding a Master's degree from a standard college, or its equivalent." But as usual the College was in debt with "the amount of liabilities over assets" totaling $12,203.73. The Trustees recommended to the Associations at their 1930 sessions "that the churches put the College in their budget[s] for a definite amount to be paid each year toward reducing the indebtedness and paying current expenses until such time as an adequate endowment shall be provided. . . ." They also recommended "that the respective Associations endorse the movement to encourage farmers to plant and cultivate one acre of cotton for the use and benefit of Boiling Springs Junior College, the Trustees to furnish the fertilizer and planting seed, and the tenant to have the seed for the expense of ginning and cultivating and delivering the cotton to Boiling Springs." The women too were not to be left out. The Trustees, therefore, recommended "that the Associations endorse the movement inaugurated by the women to contribute a chicken for the purpose of procuring books for the library." But if not in life, then in death the members of the Associations were urged to provide for the College by providing bequests in their wills to increase the badly needed endowment of the College.

The fourth academic year of the College began on the first day of September, 1931, with 68 college and 93 high school students. There were now nine Departments, all headed by teachers holding M.A. degrees or better. The financial depression, however, continued; and the College, like individuals, was forced to economize. Football, described as "by far the most expensive sport," was discontinued for the school year, although inter-collegiate basketball and baseball were not dropped. The athletic program was directed by Coach B. G. Rackley, who from 1929 to the spring of 1931 had been assisted by Assistant Physical Education Director Broadus "Pop" Simmons. In the fall of 1930, Boiling Springs Junior College won the Junior College Football Championship. The next year, as far as Boiling Springs Junior College was concerned, the Great Depression was awarded the bays.

President Zeno Wall made the Christian Education Report and the report on the College at the meeting of the Associations in 1931. Even if the depression had not seriously taken its toll of the student body, the depression had made it necessary for the fledgling College to rely for the first time upon its own wings and the three sponsoring Associations. The North Carolina Baptist State Convention, now overburdened with debt, turned the College back to the Gaston, Kings Mountain, and Sandy Run Associations. Dr. Wall asked, "Shall we permit it to die, or shall we, like the communities where the other Baptist schools are located, get back of it in such a way as to warrant its life and unselfishness?" The Associations, so he made quite clear, must answer. The faculty—"one of the most capable and consecrated faculties to be found in any school, a faculty, each member of which is actually sacrificing to make the school go"—had already done their part in reducing voluntarily their meager salaries three hundred dollars. Economy, Dr. Wall pointed out, was being practiced in every place, but the situation was still serious.

The Cleveland Star, March 23, 1932, announced the appointment of the Reverend J. L. Jenkins, pastor of the Boiling Springs Baptist Church, to the presidency of the College, succeeding Dr. Wall. Mr. Jenkins was to assume his duties at the close of the academic year late in May or the first of June. Mr. Jenkins, however, made it clear to the Trustees that he would accept the presidency only on a temporary basis—only "until they could secure a permanent man." The position carried no salary, only traveling expenses. On Founders' Day in October President Jenkins was formally installed. To be sure the College lacked money, but President Jenkins also found the physical plant in sore need of repair. The water system was inadequate; the well and the pump in front of what is now known as the Huggins-Curtis Building furnished barely enough water. Seventy leaks were found in the various buildings, not to mention the broken pipes and leaking faucets. For years junk had been accumulating under the buildings until over a car load was finally removed. Boys' Dormitory, "The Barn," as it was called, was almost that in reality; it badly needed repairs.

The financial situation of the College became increasingly serious with each passing day. The Trustees knew that they must formulate a realistic yet definite and firm financial policy—one that they meant to adhere to tenaciously. They met on April 29, 1932, and worked out their desperate but determined policy. First of all, the College must live within its income; this was the *sine qua non*. It only remained then to decide how the income, such as it may be, was to be spent. Operating expenses, of course, must be paid—that is, all except teachers' salaries. Ten per cent of the net balance was to be applied on the indebtedness. The teachers were to be paid out of any balance of income which might remain after the other operating expenses were taken care of. If what was left was sufficient to pay teachers' salaries in full, well and good. If not, then the funds remaining were to be distributed pro rata among the teachers on the basis of the salaries fixed in the contracts. The Trustees did not wish to be held personally responsible for teachers' salaries—in fact, would not be; and they voted "that the teachers be so instructed." They would not even set the likely-not-to-be-paid salaries; President Jenkins and W. L. Hicks, the Business Manager, were assigned this task.

The teachers often became restless because of their meager salaries; but there were teachers with Ph.D. degrees waiting to take their places if they left, teachers who were willing to teach in exchange for a place to live and eat. At one time some of the Trustees were in favor of turning the school over to the State, but there were always a few who held out, although at times, no doubt, it seemed futile to hope to carry on. Had it not been for E. B.

Hamrick, a Boiling Springs merchant, the school surely would have closed. At one time he marked $4,000 off his books which the College owed him, and for almost one year he fed the student body free of charge. "If it had not been for Brother E. B. Hamrick and Boiling Springs Church," President Jenkins has since informed the author, "the College would have closed down for good." But in spite of the appalling lack of funds, from 32 to 35 athletic scholarships were given, an apparently unjustifiable expenditure which caused an understandable dissatisfaction among the faculty members. As President Jenkins later said, "We won championships two years in football at the expense of teachers' salaries."

In the midst of these dark days, Professor Huggins, first Principal of the Boiling Springs High School and first Dean of Boiling Springs Junior College, died on April 19, 1932. Two days later, the Trustees paid Professor Huggins the highest tribute possible, declaring that to Professor Huggins, "more than to any other man or group of men" who had been attached to the institution, Boiling Springs High School and Junior College was indebted for its "material, intellectual, and spiritual achievement." Early the next month—May 3, 1932—the Trustees adopted the following resolution:

> The Board of Trustees of Boiling Springs Junior College, in recognition of a quarter of a century of distinguished and sacrificial service by Professor James Dwyre Huggins to the High School and College and through them to the general interest of Christian education, culture, and service for Christ and humanity to both the regions at home and abroad, being ever mindful of his noble ideals, unselfish spirit, charming personality, broad intellect, unimpeachable character, kindly sympathetic heart and broad vision of life, desire to give expression to and to publish abroad their cherished memory of his great spirit and to bear testimony to his noble life's achievements.

No death in the official family of the institution had ever left such a vacuum. Many students could hardly conceive of the College without Professor Huggins. There was even some talk of burying him on the campus in front of the building that now bears his name. But wisdom prevailed over sentiment, and he was laid to rest in the Boiling Springs Cemetery.

The Trustees found themselves in a position that became increasingly unenviable. The Gaston Association decided to leave the College to the other Associations. The Executive Committee of the Trustees was advised by the Business Manager of the College on September 7, 1932, that the College faced a law suit. Some teachers of the 1931-1932 faculty who had not been re-elected for the 1932-1933 academic year had employed a lawyer in Charlotte and were entering suit for salary due them. At the Kings Mountain and Sandy Run Associational meetings, the Trustees reminded the delegates of the money that they had been authorized and directed "to borrow to procure the necessary equipment to standardize the school." The money was now due the bank and others, and the bank had called its loan, now amounting to $1800. The College, however, had now "met all requirements of the Standard of the Association of Southern Colleges and Secondary Schools," the Associations were told, "except an income of $10,000 over and above tuition fees." This would have been some little consolation to the harassed Trustees if it had not been that the "College closed its [fiscal] year June 30, 1932, with a considerable deficit in operating expenses," most of which it owed "to its faithful teachers." The Trustees recommended "that each church of the two Associations designate at the earliest practical date a fixed sum which it will raise during the next year, at such time or times and in such ways as it may elect, for the aid of Boiling Springs Junior College." A year later, however, the loan due the bank had not been paid, and now the "private parties" from whom money had been borrowed were also calling their loans. The Trustees needed $4500 badly and quickly.

On the twenty-second day of May, 1933, the Trustees

reaffirmed their financial policy which they first passed on April 29, 1932. At their June, 1933, meeting, the Trustees appointed Miss Etta Curtis Alumni Secretary at a yearly salary of $300 and room and board. Her salary, however, was to be pro rated like the salary of the teachers if the College ended the year with a deficit. Miss Curtis was to keep in touch with the alumni under the over-all direction of the President and Business Manager, who could, if they saw fit, assign her additional duties. The financial policy of the Trustees was put to a test at the annual meeting of the Board on May 21, 1934. A faculty couple appeared before the Board and "asked for a full settlement of back salary at once." However, on a motion by the Reverend J. A. Hunnicutt, seconded by the Reverend J. W. Suttle, the Board voted to "adhere to the policy laid down by the Board last year and that the Finance Committee so instruct them and any others making similar requests."

On March 7, 1935, President J. L. Jenkins submitted his resignation to the Executive Committee of the Trustees, asking that he be relieved of the duties of the presidency at the close of the academic year. The Trustees were once again faced with the duty of finding a man—a suitable man—who would accept the position. The presidency was offered to the Reverend C. A. Maddrey, pastor of the First Baptist Church of Spindale, N. C., at a salary of $1600 a year, a home, and $400 for traveling expenses; but Mr. Maddrey declined the offer. On May 21, 1935, the Faculty Committee, following a motion by the Reverend J. W. Suttle, was instructed to secure A. C. Lovelace as President, if he would accept.

President Jenkins, not wishing his successor to be embarrassed by a situation that had been smarting him, asked "for a stand to be taken on athletics and so inform the incoming President." The Trustees decided that the policy of awarding athletic scholarships would be continued but that they would "be limited to $26 for any one student regardless of how many different teams he makes."

A. C. Lovelace did accept the presidency but resigned in April of 1936, his resignation to take effect after the close of the academic year. He, like his predecessor, found the College buildings badly in need of repair. He reported to the Trustees at their semi-annual meeting on January 28, 1936, that all rooms on the second floor of the Girls' Dormitory badly needed new ceilings and floors, that the walls needed refinishing, and that the roof of the Memorial Building must be repaired.

Following the resignation of President Lovelace, the College faced its darkest hour. It faced a crisis that many despaired of overcoming. At the annual meeting of the Board of Trustees, May 18, 1936, a special committee—composed of B. T. Falls, J. U. Rollins, G. V. Hawkins, Mrs. Rush Stroup, President A. C. Lovelace, and the Reverend J. A. Hunnicutt—reported. The College had been dropped from the accredited list by the North Carolina Department of Public Instruction, and the special committee "unanimously agreed that Boiling Springs Junior College cannot open next fall unless it is a regular standard Junior College." But in any event, at least $6000 must be available to enable the College to operate. If the Board *could* meet these conditions, the special committee recommended that provisions be made to open the next fall as usual. B. T. Falls, however, made a motion that the College suspend operation—a motion that received a second from S. H. Austell—but the motion failed to carry.

The College then *would* continue—that is, if some way could be found to finance it. A. W. McMurry made a motion at the same meeting that the Trustees, within the next two weeks, see what could be done toward raising $10,000 to liquidate the indebtedness of the College. He suggested that the churches be asked to send in 50 per cent of their mission contributions to help run the school and that the Board meet again on June 1 to map out future plans. His motion carried.

The future plans included a meeting of representatives

of the Board—President A. C. Lovelace, the Reverend J. L.
Jenkins, the Reverend Rush Padgett, and E. B. Hamrick—
with Dr. Clyde A. Erwin, Dr. James E. Hillman, and Dr.
J. Henry Highsmith of the North Carolina Department
of Public Instruction on June 3, 1936. The College *had*
to secure accreditation, if at all possible. The representatives of the Board "guaranteed" an income of $10,000,
the "sum to be paid by the Kings Mountain and Sandy
Run Association, one or both," and "to be available for
operation of the school." They also agreed, according to
a report from Dr. J. Henry Highsmith read to the Trustees by President Lovelace at the First Baptist Church of
Shelby, June 22, 1936, that five teachers with Master's
degrees would be employed as Heads of five Departments—
English, Mathematics, Science, Social Studies, and Foreign
Language—and that the salaries of the teachers would
"not, in any case, be less than that of a Class A teacher's
under the State Salary Schedule for public school teachers
plus 25 per cent. In the case of a Class A-8 teacher, the
amount would be $1215 on the basis of $108 a month for
nine months plus 25 per cent." This was a far cry from
the $35 plus room and board which the faculty received
in 1935-36. According to the report, laboratory equipment, valued at not less than $2000 for each of the sciences
taught, must be provided and the present laboratories
renovated "or other satisfactory space provided [with]
. . . modern equipment, including laboratory tables and
chairs." The College must secure a full-time librarian, who
was to be paid on the same basis as the regular teachers,
and at least $500 must be spent on books for the library.
And these were not all—any other requirements set up in
the Standards for Junior Colleges must "be faithfully observed." The representatives of the Board had agreed to
the stipulations laid down by Drs. Erwin, Hillman, and
Highsmith. Only so could the College have its accreditation extended another year. It was now up to the Board.
Could it possibly hope to meet these specific requirements?
Board member Dr. W. A. Ayers asked, "When shall the

College be required to meet all the requirements outlined by Dr. Highsmith in order to be standard?" President Lovelace replied, "Before the end of the school term of 1936-1937 all requirements must be met if the school remains on the standard." No doubt with trepidation and unwarranted hope, the Trustees ordered the copies of the agreement signed and one copy returned to Dr. Highsmith. They were simply following the advice of Franklin Delano Roosevelt: "When you come to the end of your rope, tie a knot and hang on."

The College *would* continue to struggle for another year, at least. The Board was unconsciously demonstrating Oscar Wilde's observation, "The world is divided into two classes: those who believe the incredible, and those who do the improbable." But on the earlier assumption that it was surely going to close, no catalogue was published in the spring of 1936. The College now had no President; and nobody, consequently, had been busy during the summer securing a faculty or students for the coming academic year. It was not until late summer—August 24 to be exact—that the Board had a special called meeting to consider a new President. A good deal of discussion ensued, but a motion by M. A. Spangler that "the Trustees empower the Chairman to appoint a committee of three and give them power to employ Dr. George Burnett of Marshall, Texas, to be President of Boiling Springs Junior College" carried.

George Jackson Burnett accepted the presidency of the College at a salary of $2000. President Burnett held both the A.B. and M.A. degrees from Bethel College. From 1907-1923, he was President of Tennessee College for Women. For two years, 1915-1917, he was President of the Tennessee Baptist State Convention. For one year, he was Vice-President of the Southern Baptist Convention, and for three and one-half years, Associate Secretary of the Baptist Brotherhood of the South. President Burnett brought to the presidency of the College a wealth of ex-

MISS ETTA CURTIS
(1858-1940)

perience in both college administration and denominational work—experience which stood him in good stead. He was an indefatigable man; at times he worked all night. He was bookkeeper, bursar, teacher, and President—everything except librarian and dietitian.

Things that needed to be done were legion. There was the problem of teacher load. Records were not properly kept. President Burnett impressed Professor Hubert Dixon into service to help with the internal affairs of the College. By the end of the academic year in the spring of 1937, Professor Dixon had worked out an absence system and had so impressed the President with his efficiency and acumen that, on the President's recommendation, Professor Dixon was made Dean of the College. President Burnett felt that, if he could strengthen the churches, they would put the College in their budgets. He also recommended to the Trustees, after his first year, that the total cost to a student for an academic year at Boiling Springs Junior College be raised to $270—a hike in total expenses of $60. That additional $60, however, was to be a trading proposition whereby the President hoped to get the furnace fired and the grass cut. Every student was to be offered a job.

President Burnett set up a salary scale which he proposed to meet. The faculty was to receive $50 a month—perhaps less than a third of the State Salary Scale plus 25 per cent which the Trustees had indicated they hoped to pay. There was no doubt now that the College's accreditation with the North Carolina State Department of Public Instruction would be lost. In fact, the Trustees further called upon President Burnett to reduce expenses, and he cut salaries, including his own, by 10 per cent. The President, however, did get the Trustees to agree, so he thought, that, in the event of a surplus at the end of the year which would justify it, the teachers would get a 10 per cent raise, rather than a cut. There was such a surplus, but the Trustees now refused to regard themselves bound to pay anything except the base amount of $50. President Burnett argued that the money was available and that it was owed to the faculty, and he urged the faculty to push *en masse* for what he felt to be due them, but to no avail. The faculty settled for the base amount, which was, after all, 10 per cent more than at one time they expected to get.

President Burnett changed the College from the semester to the quarter system in 1937. The College needed students badly; and, the President reasoned, on the quarter system there would be one more time for students to enter during an academic year than was formerly the case. Then, too, on the quarter system there would be no Saturday classes, and students could work or go home on the weekends.

President Burnett believed strongly in an educated ministry, and he kept adding courses for ministers who lacked a formal education. At one time, there were twenty-three preachers who had not finished high school attending classes at Boiling Springs Junior College.

Then came the Great Conflagration. Just after midnight on the twelfth of November, 1937, the Memorial Building burned. There were four rooms in the basement of the building and two on the main floor in which at least fifteen boys lived. The upper floors were used by the State-supported Boiling Springs High School. The Memorial Building was completely gutted since there was no steel at all in the building. There stood only the smoke blackened walls.

At three o'clock that morning, President Burnett called a faculty meeting and announced that there would be no college classes the rest of that week. The fire had damaged the heating plant to such an extent that it could not be used. The High School shortly thereafter moved into the Boiling Springs Baptist Church. The College resumed its classes the next week in the literary society halls, the dining hall, and the library. The chemistry and biology laboratories were set up in an old frame building, a vacated store, near the old post office. Richard M. Rice was not only coach and teacher of biology and chemistry, but luckily he was something of a plumber as well. The old building had running water and some shelves and tables, and a few microscopes had been rescued from the fire. Before long Professor Rice was again about his task of teaching the natural sciences. The College carried about $15,000 in insurance on the Memorial Building. The Trustees voted to take part of the money received from the insurance and pay off the $6000 note on the gymnasium. With the remainder, they had enough to pay off about one-fourth of the debt of the College. The Trustees decided that they would make a bold attempt to get the College out of debt. Consequently, they decided to ask the creditors of the College if they would settle for twenty-five cents on the dollar. President Burnett did not approve of the action of the Board of Trustees, but he agreed reluctantly to see the creditors and to lay the Board's proposition before them.

It was the Trustees' financial policies and the President's notions of financial propriety which eventually led to a break between the Board and the President. For one thing, President Burnett decided to halt the National Youth Administration program on the campus. No longer, he decided, would Boiling Springs Junior College students receive money from the Federal Government. Although the N.Y.A. program was one aspect of the Roosevelt Administration's National Recovery Program and the idea back of it was to "prime the college pumps" and keep the students in the colleges, President Burnett quite likely felt that the historic Baptist principle of the separation of church and state was being compromised on the grounds of expediency. Some of the Trustees, however, did not approve of his action nor his position on the matter. Then on July 4, 1938, the Trustees employed J. L. Lovelace at a salary of $40 per month and traveling expenses to assist the President in collecting past due student accounts and "to secure all possible information concerning the security of the balance." Mr. Lovelace was elected without President Burnett's consent, and the President resigned. Judge E. Yates Webb, Chairman of the Board, said to him, "I'm

amazed. We thought we were doing this to give you help."
President Burnett's contention was that the College could
not afford to pay an extra man at that time. The Trustees,
however, refused to accept the resignation, and President
Burnett agreed to stay on. Later, however, financial dis-
agreements, like Hydra's heads, arose and sparked the
animous that led to another resignation of President Burnett. This one the Trustees did accept. As he later informed the author, when asked about the conditions under
which he left the presidency of the College, "The Trustees
made me mad when they took the management of the
money out of my hands. I moved to Gaffney, S. C., and
accepted work with Limestone College."

At a called meeting of the Board of Trustees on February 23, 1939, Judge E. Yates Webb read President Burnett's resignation, which was to take effect March 1, 1939.
The Board requested the Reverend J. W. Suttle, D. F.
Hord, and the Reverend W. P. Biggerstaff "to draw up
resolutions of respect for the fine work done at the College
and in the field by Dr. Burnett." But, alas, again the College was without a President. At the February 23 meeting,
Judge Webb appointed the Reverend T. H. Parris, J. U.
Rollins, A. W. McMurry, and J. F. Lutz to a committee
to recommend "some capable person to fill out the balance
of the school year as President." Before the meeting ad-
journed, the committee presented the following recommendation: "We, the Nominating Committee, after due
consideration, unanimously recommend that Rev. J. L.
Jenkins be named temporary President, to be assisted by
Professor Hubert Dixon and Rev. W. W. Davidson, [and]
to work in cooperation with the Treasurer, J. L. Lovelace.
We also recommend that the Chairman of the Board name
a committee of four, two from [the] Kings Mountain and
two from [the] Sandy Run Associations, to go and consult
with the above nominees in regard to the division of the
work, compensation, *etc.*" At the same meeting, Chairman
Webb appointed a committee—composed of the Reverend
W. P. Biggerstaff, Chairman, W. L. Hicks, Mrs. John W.

Wacaster, A. W. McMurry, T. T. Long, D. F. Hord, and Dr. W. A. Ayers—to recommend a President, whose work would begin with the academic year 1939-40.

On the fifth day of May, the Trustees met again in a called meeting to receive the report of the Nominating Committee appointed six weeks before. Chairman Biggerstaff could not be present at this meeting, and his letter recommending that the Reverend John R. Cantrell be elected President was read by Judge Webb, after which A. W. McMurry made the Committee's report. During the previous summer Mr. Cantrell had conducted a revival meeting at the Boiling Springs Church at which time he became interested in the College. He had graduated from Boiling Springs High School in 1919 and had received the A.B. degree from Wake Forest College in 1924; and from 1928 to 1931, he had served as an evangelist with the North Carolina Baptist Mission Board. His salary as President was set at $2000 a year, plus an expense allowance, the amount of which the Executive Committee of the Trustees was to decide upon later. In addition, he was to be provided with a home and utilities.

President Cantrell became interested in beautifying the College campus. He set out trees and shrubbery, constructed walks, planted iris along the walks, built a lily pond, and added a front porch to the Boys' Dormitory. Something too needed to be done to improve the appearance of the gymnasium—a storm-sheeted, weather-boarded, wooden frame building. Cleveland County had an abundance of rocks. The fields were strewn with them, and President Cantrell knew some rock masons. As he was able to raise the money, he paid people to haul loads of rocks to the campus, and he set the rock masons to work on a project which ultimately cost $7000. The result was that the gymnasium was completely rock-veneered.

But the College was merely dragging on—not dead, although some of the Trustees still feared it would die; yet no one would say that it was vibrantly alive. Again, as always, it was money and more money that was needed. The Trustees turned to Horace Easom, Director of Religious Education and Music at Shelby's First Baptist Church. They would give him 5 per cent of all the funds he collected, if he would only collect funds for the College. Mr. Easom saw the weaknesses inherent in such an arrangement and plainly told the Trustees that such an arrangement would defeat a money-raising campaign. He would take no money; but, when it was all over, if they wished to offer him an expenses-paid vacation at Myrtle Beach, S. C., that he would take.

Horace Easom was a shrewd money raiser, a student of human nature, and a meticulous, calculating planner. He knew the propensity of people to go along with a winner. He insisted, therefore, that, if the campaign were to succeed, a part of it must be underwritten before the campaign was launched. He recruited Mal Spangler, and together they called upon some of the moneyed friends of the College. They asked E. B. Hamrick for $10,000. "That's too much for me," he said. "Well, then," they pressed, "how about $10,000 for you and all your boys." Mr. Hamrick agreed that *that* was different, and he gave $10,-000. They also asked A. W. McMurry and S. A. McMurry for $10,000.

The plans were carefully and quietly laid; but when conditions were right, the Greater Boiling Springs Junior College Campaign was publicly announced with a great deal of fanfare. The *Cleveland Times* brought out an EXTRA edition on October 21, 1941, to break the news. In a front page editorial, Chairman Easom is declared to have said "that a movement is beginning which will make Boiling Springs College a million-dollar institution in ten years." Hope was expressed that the people of the area would "rally in a wonderful way to this great movement for a permanent and efficient Christian college in our midst." The Campaign, the newspaper reported, would seek to raise $100,000—$40,000 of which had already been subscribed by seventeen donors in amounts of $10,000, $5,000, $2,000, and $1,000. Along with Chairman Easom and his Associate Chairman Mal Spangler, A. W. McMurry had agreed to act as Chairman of the Steering Committee, and C. Rush Hamrick was to be his Associate Chairman. In the *Cleveland Times* EXTRA, Chairman Easom outlined the six needs that he said would have to be realized if the College were to be a success. First, the College needed $10,000 in order to become standardized. In the second place, $5,000 was needed to landscape and beautify the campus. Thirdly, to finish the Administration Building would take $15,000; and, fourthly, another $15,000 would be required to modernize and refurnish the present buildings. And, in the fifth place, $30,000 would be necessary to build a proposed new dormitory with twenty-five rooms; and, lastly, the College needed $25,000 as a start on an endowment fund.

Two days later, the *Cleveland Times* of October 23 called attention to the meeting of the Kings Mountain Association that convened that morning at the Elizabeth Church. Headlining the morning session was to be an hour and a half discussion of the $100,000 Greater Boiling Springs Junior College Campaign. A week later the *Times* reported a barbecue and a rally attended by "a large congregation of supporters" and held in the College gymnasium at which "former Governor Clyde R. Hoey, in an after-dinner speech, praised the College for the development of the school and what it had done for boys and girls in this section."

On the fourth of December, 1941, the *Times* announced that Seaton A. Washburn, then 81 years of age and founder of Shelby's Washburn Hardware Store, had verified reports that he planned to give the College a library building, "separate and apart from the financial campaign." It was to be erected on some land recently donated to the College by the Boiling Springs Baptist Church and was to be in memory of the Washburn family in general but especially in memory of Mr. Washburn's wife, now deceased, and

their two daughters, Miss Olin Washburn and Mrs. Mae
Washburn McMurry.

Expansion and progress now became the shibboleths of
the day. Campaign Chairman Easom could not sleep because of his concern over the Lilliputian campus of the
expanding College. It must have more land, and to E. B.
Hamrick again went Mr. Easom. The Boiling Springs merchant's generosity was exceeded only by his love for the
College. "Get all the land you want," he said. "Boys, get
plenty." And with practical and farsighted "greediness"
commensurate with the benevolence of the donor, Chairman Easom did just that.

Early in 1942, Mr. Easom wrote former North Carolina
Governor O. Max Gardner and sent him a copy of the
plans for a Greater Boiling Springs Junior College. This
was not the first time Governor Gardner had had the needs
of the College brought to his attention. In the late thirties
President George J. Burnett discussed with Governor
Gardner the College's need of $600,000; and, according to
President Burnett, "Governor Gardner promised to help."
Within a week after his letter was written, Mr. Easom got
a two-paged, single-spaced letter from Governor Gardner,
acquainting him with the fact that the Governor had already made his commitments for the year, but that he
would give $1000. Governor Gardner, however, asked Mr.
Easom to keep in contact with him. Consequently, ninety
days later Mr. Easom again wrote Governor Gardner; and
a little later, when the Governor came home to Shelby, he
asked Mr. Easom to come over to the Cleveland Cloth Mill.
By this time, Governor Gardner, so it seems, had fairly
definitely decided to back the College financially. "I've
made all the money I want to make," he said. "Now I
want a project." Boiling Springs Junior College seems to
have been the project he wanted. But what if he should
not live to see the project through to completion? Governor Gardner got his three sons—James Webb, Ralph, and
Max, Jr.—in his car and drove the nine miles from Shelby

out to Boiling Springs. He asked his sons if they would see the project through if he should not live to see it completed. They promised they would.

Early in the summer of 1942, Governor Gardner gave the College a gift of $10,000 to make available twenty-five scholarships to young men and women of the area. His reason, as he pointed out some time later, was to see if the College could attract better students, for he felt that it was failing in its efforts to secure "the best and most ambitious material as students." In a letter to Judge E. Yates Webb, Chairman of the Board of Trustees, Governor Gardner explained the use to which his gift was to be put:

I desire through you to offer to the Board of Trustees the sum of $10,000, payable as follows: $5,000 on or before September 1, 1942, and $5,000 on or before September 1, 1943.

The purpose of this gift, if the Board of Trustees approves, is to credit 25 cash scholarships for a period of two years for the use and benefit of worthy students attending Boiling Springs Junior College during the college years of 1942-43 and 1943-44; each scholarship to consist of $200 in cash, or its equivalent in board, tuition or fees; 20 of said scholarships to be awarded to 20 young men or women, high school graduates of Cleveland County, North Carolina, and five to be awarded to five young men or women of Rutherford County, North Carolina; said $10,000 to be kept by said Board of Trustees as a separate fund and to be used for no other purpose.

....

I have great faith in Boiling Springs Junior College and its high value to the people of our section. I am genuinely proud of the splendid contribution this institution has made to the life of this section, and I believe in the future it is capable of doing a great deal more than in the past, provided it continues to receive the sympathetic support and loyalty of our people.

The *Cleveland Times*, June 11, 1942, revealed that for a week past young men and women from Cleveland County had been applying at the rate of more than two each day for one of the twenty scholarships available to them.

Shortly thereafter Governor Gardner received the following letter from his close friend Franklin D. Roosevelt, President of the United States:

The White House
Washington

June 23, 1942

Dear Max:

I want to congratulate you on the farsighted vision which prompted your generous gift of ten thousand dollars to establish scholarships for promising boys and girls in the Boiling Springs Junior College.

This is an act of faith in the future which should be an inspiration to friends of education everywhere. I am glad to know, also, that it is your purpose, in establishing this foundation, to encourage young men and women who are to be its beneficiaries to acquire skill of hand while pursuing the liberal arts. Since the college is located in the center of an industrial-agricultural area, the training which the scholarships will afford should be of real value to the communities from which the students are drawn.

I hope the undertaking meets with the success which its high purpose merits.

Very sincerely yours,
(signed)   Franklin D. Roosevelt

Honorable O. Max Gardner
Suite 1126
Woodward Building
Washington, D. C.

While he was Governor of North Carolina, O. Max Gardner came to know Franklin D. Roosevelt, then Governor of New York. To Governor Gardner goes the honor and distinction of having suggested to Democratic Nominee Franklin D. Roosevelt the idea of the New Deal. On July 22, 1932, just after Roosevelt's nomination, Governor Gardner wrote him a letter in which he outlined the left-of-center policy which Roosevelt later followed:

It is my opinion that the American people are on the move, and I firmly believe that your liberalism, if you go far enough, is bound to have a stabilizing effect in its appeal to the ultimate hope of the nation. If I were you, I would become more liberal because I tell you the masses are marching; and if we are to save this nation, it has got to be saved by the liberal interpretations of the sentiments now ruling in the hearts of men.

I am satisfied that we are in the day of a new deal and that many of our preconceived ideas and formulas are going to be thrown into the discard. We are more than blind if we think the American people will stand hitched to the status quo. The camp fires of the past are being abandoned and the frontiers of thinking have extended beyond the limit heretofore held sacred by the conservative minds of this country.

When Roosevelt went to Washington in 1933, Max Gardner went, too. He opened a law office, but simultaneously resigned from the Democratic National Committee, feeling that politics and a personal law practice did not mix. In spite of the fact that Max Gardner had represented Coca-Cola, Pan-American Airways, and various shipping lines, he became more liberal with the years. President Roosevelt offered him several jobs, but he turned them down, preferring to spend his spare time—if he could find any—on his front porch in Shelby, rocking in an old chair that the Negroes of Shelby gave him thirty-five years before as a wedding present when he and Miss Faye Webb were wed.

Later, however, the siren call of politics proved too much for him or perchance a strong sense of duty motivated his action, and he finally yielded to the urging of his old friend, Secretary of the Treasury Vinson, to become Under Secretary of the Treasury; and President Harry S. Truman made one of his best appointments.

But in spite of it all, Max Gardner never lost his Southern charm, chivalric touch, and genial humor. One day he was talking to the Duchess of Windsor, who exclaimed, "Oh, it was so nice at Annapolis, just as beautiful and charming as in the old days. It hasn't changed a bit."

Governor Gardner replied, "Lady, there is nothing remarkable about the unchanged beauty of Annapolis. I just heard a friend of yours remark that he hadn't seen you for ten years and that you were just as lovely and beautiful and unchanged as before you met the King of England."

The Duchess countered, "I wish I could believe you. But that's just the old blarney of the South."

"My dear," said he, "you can always believe the South-

ern politician any time except when he is running for
office. And, since I am not a candidate, you must believe
me also when I tell you that when we talk with you and
the Duke, we feel we are talking in the presence of history."

4

Gardner-Webb College— 1942-1956

T HIS WAS the man—Oliver Max Gardner— who in 1942, not only began to pour his money into Boiling Springs Junior College, but began also to devote his energies and to give his time, along with others, in guiding and strengthening the College, and whose name the College was soon to bear.

In June of 1942, Dr. George W. Truett, pastor of the First Baptist Church of Dallas, Texas, conducted a ten-day revival meeting in the Shelby Armory, under the sponsorship of the First Baptist Church of Shelby. An estimated 30,000 people crowded into the Armory during the ten-day meeting to hear the world's most renown Baptist minister. On June 15, two days before the close of the revival, a luncheon was held in Shelby's Hotel Charles to which were invited the Trustees of Boiling Springs Junior College and their wives and all pastors of the Kings Mountain and Sandy Run Associations and their wives. Dr. and Mrs. Truett were also present. Dr. Truett spoke. It was a high hour. Dr. Zeno Wall, pastor of the First Baptist Church of Shelby, presided at the luncheon. The men present were asked to stay for a business meeting following the luncheon, but the Reverend John W. Suttle saw no reason why the wives should not stay too, and he said so. It was at this meeting, following Dr. Truett's message, that Chairman of the Greater Boiling Springs Junior College Campaign, Horace Easom, suggested that the College's name be changed to Gardner-Webb College in honor of two of Cleveland County's outstanding families. The Reverend John W. Suttle made a motion that the name be changed; Dr. W. A. Ayers, pastor of the First Baptist Church of Forest City, N. C., seconded the motion with a speech; and those present unanimously approved the motion.

Other significant steps were also being taken. The *Cleveland Times*, June 11, 1942—four days before the name of the College was changed—announced the appointment of a committee by Judge E. Yates Webb, Chairman of the Board of Trustees, to arrange "for a survey of the local College's needs, [the survey] to be made by outstanding educators of North Carolina." Governor Gardner headed the committee. The survey, as originally planned, was to have been made by Dr. Frank Porter Graham, President of the Greater University of North Carolina, Dr. J. Henry Highsmith of the North Carolina Department of Public Instruction, Chancellor J. W. Harrelson of North Carolina State College, President A. Carlyle Campbell of Meredith College, and President Thurman D. Kitchin of Wake Forest College. Presidents Graham and Campbell, however, were not on the Survey Committee as it was ultimately constituted. Dr. Highsmith was Chairman; and with him on the Survey Committee were Chancellor Harrelson, Professor Claude Teague of the Woman's College of the University of North Carolina, President Kitchin of Wake Forest, and Dr. Fred W. Morrison, Governor Gardner's law partner.

In order to make clear his interest in the College, Governor Gardner wrote a letter to the Survey Committee:

I am also writing this letter on my own behalf, in order that your Committee may know of my interest in this institution. Since Boiling Springs High School was organized in 1905, I have followed it with interest, but I have never [before] been identified with this institution either first as a High School or later as a College.

When the campaign to raise $100,000 for this College was started in 1941, I made a contribution of $1000 to the fund. I had previously given small amounts to the school. Some months ago I was requested to make a further contribution to the fund. After careful consideration, I declined to do this; but as an alternative, I gave 25 scholarships of $200 each for a period of two years to worthy boys and girls of Cleveland and Rutherford Counties. My reason for doing this was that I felt the institution was not succeeding in its effort to secure the best and most ambitious material as students. I wanted for a period of two years, more or less as an experiment, to see if this plan would keep the institution alive as a going concern in order that all of those interested in it might have a reasonable period for studying its future possibilities or lack of possibilities.

The change of the name of the institution from Boiling Springs College to Gardner-Webb Junior College has no relation to my interest in the institution and will not influence my attitude with respect to its future. When I gave the scholarships, the name of the institution was Boiling Springs College. I would have been just as interested in helping maintain it during the experimental period I had in mind if its name had not been changed. The Board of Trustees thought otherwise, and unanimously voted to change the name to honor the Gardner and Webb families of Cleveland and Rutherford Counties.

If your survey is approved by the Board of Trustees and receives its support, I shall be happy within my limited means to co-operate with the Board, the supporting churches, and the institution's friends to make it worthy of the faith of its founders and a creditable contribution to the development of Christian education in Cleveland and adjoining counties.

I have known of the hard and desperate struggle of this institution to become a Junior College. Frankly, I have been impressed with the fact that it refused to die. Yet I have never deluded myself with the idea that I, as an individual, possessed the capacity or means to make it live. I am firmly of the opinion that there is a need for a strong junior college in this broad and prosperous community and that there are abundant means to support it provided its friends will take a real and genuine interest in it.

I sincerely hope your study will find that this College has a future and is worthy to live, and that your report will merit and receive the generous and hearty support of all friends of this College everywhere.

Faithfully yours,
O. Max Gardner, Chairman

The Survey Committee did find the College "worthy to live," but its report of November 12, 1942, nevertheless, made some very definite recommendations about its future life. "As soon as possible," the report stated, "a new President should be secured, such person being fully qualified to administer the affairs of a junior college. He should be a man who has had academic and professional training, with a Bachelor of Arts degree and with at least two years of graduate study in an institution of recognized standing. He should," the report continued, "possess acceptable personal and social traits, attractive personality and should have good judgment and ability to get along with folks. Satisfactory gift as a public speaker is highly desirable. He should be a man of such character and proven ability that he would be recognized by people in academic circles." The faculty should be composed of academically and professionally trained men and women, who are "in full sympathy with the aims and purposes of Gardner-Webb College in the matter of Christian education." The student body, the report further recommended, should be increased to 300 as soon as possible, and "every effort [should] be made to meet the cultural and vocational needs of the students. . . . This means that academic subjects should be offered, particularly for those who expect to enter the third year of some senior or four-year college. In addition to this, as full opportunity as possible should be given for vocational training, including agriculture, dairying, poultry raising and horticulture, home economics, industrial arts, including woodwork and metalwork." The report declared that "a definite effort should be made to offer as many terminal courses as possible." To accomplish these curricula objectives and to provide a recreation program for the students and a public relations program for the College, the institution should seek to secure $50,000 a

PHILIP LOVIN ELLIOTT
(1891-   )

year for operating the College, with "at least 50 per cent of this amount being available for instructional purposes." The physical plant should continue to be enlarged until it could adequately accommodate the student body, and definite plans should be made to meet the Standards of the North Carolina College Conference "so that Gardner-Webb Junior College may be classified as a standard junior college for the session 1942-43."

The old blackened shell of the Memorial Building had stood there, ghastly and macabre, since it went up in flame and smoke in the early morning hours of November 12, 1937, stood there looking like the carelessness of some Zoroastrian Gheber. But the portion of the walls still standing were examined and found to be sturdy and substantial. It was decided that the walls would be restored and that the Memorial Building would be rebuilt. Junius McAllister, a student experienced in building, was employed as foreman at forty-five or fifty cents an hour; and he, in turn, hired other students at fifteen cents an hour to do the work. The work went on a pace. Again it was decided not to put in steel beam supports, and the beams to support the roof—some requiring a 1000 feet of lumber—were built on the ground and hoisted into place. The building, with the exception of the auditorium, was completed by the liberal contributions of many churches and individuals. In August of 1942, $20,000 was needed to complete the auditorium; but on the last day of the month came the announcement of the Dovers' gift of $10,000 to match a like gift from Governor Gardner to finish the job. But money or no money seats for the auditorium were unavailable because of war-time rationing. Connections and know-how, though, form an unbeatable combination; and Governor Gardner, counsel for several movie houses, all of which, of course, used seats, had both. The seats arrived, and Professor Hubert Dixon and a corps of students screwed the 503 seats to the floor. Governor Gardner also secured two 35mm. movie projectors for the auditorium; a deal was worked out with a Shelby theater; and an operator, who was paid $5.00 per Saturday night, ran movies in the College auditorium.

It was decided that the restored building should be named the E. B. Hamrick Building, honoring while still alive the Boiling Springs merchant who had given food and money and land to the institution and who had served on the Board of Trustees from the beginning. The dedication service was held as part of the commencement program on May 30, 1943. Governor Gardner presided. The Reverend John W. Suttle made the presentation of the E. B. Hamrick Building and the Washburn Memorial Library, and Judge E. Yates Webb accepted the buildings. The dedicatory address was delivered by the Honorable J. Melville Broughton, Governor of North Carolina.

On April 16, 1943, in a letter addressed to Mrs. Rush Stroup, President Cantrell submitted his resignation, which, if accepted, would become effective on June 1. In a letter signed by A. W. McMurry, Chairman of the Executive Committee of the Board of Trustees, and by Mrs. Rush Stroup, Secretary, and dated April 22, 1943, President Cantrell was notified of the acceptance of his resignation. Horace Easom now became interim President until the Board could find a suitable man. The Survey Committee the winter before had sketched the qualifications of the man the Board now sought. Dean Ralph Lee of Mars Hill College turned down the presidency when it was proffered to him as President C. C. Burris of Wingate College had done the year before when he was offered the deanship of the College.

When Horace Easom was a student at Wake Forest College, he had known Phil Elliott, then also a student, but now Head of the Department of English at Western Carolina Teachers College. Mr. Easom wanted Professor Elliott at Gardner-Webb. He invited Professor Elliott to preach to the congregation at the First Baptist Church in Shelby, and the people liked him. Dr. J. Henry Highsmith, too, felt that Professor Elliott would make the College a good President, and he told Governor Gardner so. Whereupon, Professor Elliott was invited by Governor Gardner to come to Shelby to discuss the matter. He came, but went back to Cullowhee, N. C., to wrestle with his decision. On May 9, 1943, the Executive Committee of the Board of Trustees passed a resolution offering Professor Elliott the presidency of Gardner-Webb College at a salary of $2500, plus $100 traveling expenses. However, not until the middle of July did he accept the offer.

Philip Lovin Elliott, the son of a Confederate soldier who fought in the Battle of Atlanta, was born in Wayside, N. C., a little village deep among the peaks of the Smoky Mountains. At the age of eighteen and filled with a consuming desire for an education, he walked the twenty miles from Wayside to Robbinsville, where he enrolled in a small mountain academy maintained by the Presbyterians. In 1912 he went to Mars Hill, then a high school, to complete his preparation for college. While a student at Mars Hill, he was ordained as a Baptist minister; and the young Reverend Elliott began his preaching ministry by riding horseback once a month across old Bald Mountain down into Flag Pond, Tennessee, to preach to a small mountain congregation. From Mars Hill, he went to Wake Forest College in 1915, becoming there an outstanding student in English literature and journalism. Three years after enrolling in Wake Forest College, he married Miss Etta Maurine Carringer of Robbinsville. Phil Elliott's first teaching assignment was in a small, green valley deep in the heart of the Smokies at Proctor, N. C., where the Ritter Lumber Company had a sawmill village. Here in a one-room schoolhouse, made out of rough boards, he taught a four-months' subscription school for $40 a month. That pine schoolhouse has disappeared, and today close by the spot lap the mountain waters of Lake Fontana. In 1919 schoolmaster Elliott went to Bakersville, N. C., to become Principal of Mitchell Collegiate Institute, one of a chain of Baptist boarding schools at that time supported by the

Southern Baptist Home Mission Board. Here virtually under the shadow of Roan Mountain, he was principal, dean, business manager, and teacher in a school for 300 mountain boys and girls, many of whom were too poor to pay even the modest fees of the struggling mountain school. The next year, 1920, Mr. Elliott went as missionary pastor to Graham County, N. C., and one year later was made Enlistment Secretary of the North Carolina Baptist State Convention for all of Western North Carolina. In 1922, he became pastor of the Cullowhee Baptist Church; but feeling a strong urge to devote himself to Christian education, he went to Mars Hill College in 1923 as Dean and Head of the Department of English. The years between 1923 and 1930 were full ones. During those years Professor Elliott received a Master's degree in English from the University of North Carolina; and then, for more graduate study, he followed the eminent Renaissance scholar, Dr. Edwin A. Greenlaw, to Johns Hopkins University, where he worked with Professor Greenlaw and others on the Johns Hopkins' VARIORUM EDITION OF THE WORKS OF EDMUND SPENSER. Back at Mars Hill, he was made Vice-President, a position he held until 1930, when he resigned to go to Western Carolina Teachers College as Head of the English Department.

Shortly after President-elect Elliott began his work at Gardner-Webb, the Board of Trustees launched an ambitious $300,000 campaign. At a meeting of the Executive Committee of the Board on August 13, 1943, Governor Gardner made a motion that September 9, 1943, be designated as the date for the beginning of the campaign. Again Horace Easom and Mal Spangler were elected Co-Chairmen, and they were authorized "to select as their aid some one woman who would serve along with them." Wisely they chose Mrs. Rush Stroup. The three Co-Chairmen were further empowered "to select the committee, or committees, and put in action the necessary program for raising the $300,000." G. H. Roberts, formerly of the First

National Bank of Shelby but at the time of his appointment Comptroller of the Cleveland Cloth Mills of Shelby, was elected Secretary and Treasurer of what was to be known as the Memorial Fund Enlargement Campaign. A week later Governor Gardner made a report to the Board of Trustees, a report, as he put it, made "in order that each member of the Board of Trustees may be intelligently informed of the action and activities of your Executive Committee, . . . a report covering the main activities of this Committee since its creation a little more than a year ago." Governor Gardner then outlined the work of the Executive Committee for the fourteen months just past. Every debt of the College, due and past due, had been paid; and for the first time in the College's fifteen years, it would open in September free of debt and with money in the bank. A balanced budget has been adopted for the academic year 1943-44, and President-elect Elliott has assured the Committee that the College would "operate within the terms fixed by the budget." In order "to improve the standards and bring encouragement to the student body," the Committee had provided scholarships and student aid. It was also hoped, no doubt, that what Governor Gardner himself referred to as "slight salary increases to members of the faculty" might too bring some degree of encouragement to them.

Governor Gardner's report made reference also to the $150,000 spent in the fourteen months past, "money . . . spent in broad College improvements." Early in 1943, J. E. Sirrine and Company, an engineering firm of Greenville, S. C., had been engaged "to give us plans for our present needs and an outlay for the future"—plans which the Executive Committee had already approved and which called for an ultimate expenditure of nearly a half million dollars. According to Governor Gardner, "This is more than twice the size of any sum that we have ever attempted to raise in this section at one time for a charitible, religious or educational cause. It is indeed a terrific task, but there is not the slightest doubt, however, of its success on or be-

fore January 1, 1944, if all of us put our hands to the plow
and never turn back." It was hoped that Joe Lee Woodward, President of the Alumni Association, would be able
to raise $25,000 from the more than 1,000 former students
of the institution.

The plans of the J. E. Sirrine and Company provided,
at that time, for eight dormitories—six for boys and two
for girls—to cost $19,800 each. The dormitories, designed
to care for twenty-four boys or girls each, were to be built
of brick, using a colonial style of architecture. Each building was to bear the name of some outstanding citizen of
the area, living or dead, or was to be erected as a memorial
to the young men in the armed forces. The people of
Kings Mountain were to be asked to erect one of the eight
buildings as a memorial to young men from Kings Mountain who were serving their country in World War II.
The citizens of Rutherford County were to be asked to
do the same in honor of their sons. It was also hoped that
"some outstanding citizen with interests in Gaffney, S. C.,
[might] . . erect one of these dormitories as a memorial
to the late Dr. W. C. Hamrick, a native of this county,
who was born only a few miles away from this College,
and who left as a heritage to his children a record as a great
industrial statesman in South Carolina." Governor Gardner called attention to the obvious fact that the money
being collected could not be spent until after the War was
over; however, he promised "that every dollar collected
from this Campaign will be preserved and safeguarded in
every possible way."

A few days before 1943 was rung out, the Executive
Committee of the Board of Trustees met and "decided to
have an appropriate inauguration program for President
Elliott, to be held in early May," and a committee—con-
sisting of Mrs. Rush Stroup, Chairman, Horace Easom,
and Miss Margaret Young—was appointed to make the
necessary arrangements. At the same meeting, at Mr.
Easom's suggestion, the Memorial Fund Enlargement Cam-

paign, which was supposed to be concluded in a few days, was extended through 1944.

On the sixth day of May, 1944, Phil Elliott was inaugurated President of Gardner-Webb College. Twenty institutions of higher learning sent official representatives. Governor Gardner presided over the installation ceremonies, and Judge E. Yates Webb bestowed the investiture of office. President Elliott, in his inaugural address, set forth his philosophy of junior college education and indicated something of his community concept of education, which was to make Gardner-Webb somewhat unique among the junior colleges of America. "We must know our community and all its needs—vocational, civic, religious—and then build our program and constantly revise it to meet those needs," he declared. The new President sought to alleviate the fears of those who looked upon the junior college as a competitive threat to the senior colleges. "The junior college," he said, "is a distinct institution and will supplement the senior college." He pointed out what to him seemed the three great dangers from which he would seek to steer the College clear. First, it would be "easier to sell the people the idea that they have a great college here than it will [be] to build a genuinely great one." The second danger singled out was the danger of over-specialization, the danger that a student may be led "to build the super-structure of his life on too narrow an intellectual and spiritual foundation." And finally, there was the danger of attempting too rapid production. Students' minds must be allowed to be toughened through use. "Predigested intellectual and spiritual food will never produce men and women of merit." The program President Elliott had in mind would concern itself both with those students who planned later to transfer to a senior college and with those who desired only terminal education. He advocated also a program of rural adult education that would "touch the whole life of all the people, white and black." The College should, he said, "operate constructively in the civic, economic, social, political, and religious life of our people." At the center of the new President's educational philosophy stood the teacher, which Chaucer's well-known line—"And gladly wolde he learne, and gladly teche"—aptly described. The two-fold ideal of Gardner-Webb College—*Pro Deo et Humanitate*—was inscribed on the seal of the College, with the College's ultimate purpose, then, being "to produce the enlightened soul, awakened to a consciousness of eternal realities."

Dr. Frank Porter Graham, President of the Greater University of North Carolina, delivered the concluding address. "This is a day," he said, "when a mature institution becomes young in the inauguration of Philip Lovin Elliott." Dr. Graham reminded his audience that Gardner-Webb College was devoted "(1) to the development of the responsible freedom and whole personality of young men and women, (2) to the development of the rural South for its creative part in the making of America, and (3) to America's part in winning the war and the organization of peace in the world. Self-mastery comes through responsible freedom." College is a place for the mastery of both body and mind—a place where one can joyfully give himself "to the things of the mind, to develop powers of concentration, logical organization of information and ideas, accuracy and clearness of thought and statement." Yet more is needed; "moral stamina and courage for great human causes from sources deeper than body and mind," Dr. Graham said. World War II, then being bitterly fought, was, according to Dr. Graham, "not only global in extent and total in depth, but also a worldwide fascist counter-revolution against the people's revolution." The democracies needed reinvigorating, needed, to echo Thomas Wolfe, "to look homeward." "Democracy tended to provide equality of suffrage but not equality of opportunity; the freedom to worship but not the right to work; the freedom of assembly and the right of collective petition but not the freedom of the self-organization of workers and the equality of collective bargaining; corporate privilege but not agricultural parity; and political liberty but not social security against the hazards of modern society." Later Dr. Graham declared that "liberty can be raised to higher levels by the widening of social security. The old Bill of Rights can be saved only by provisions for a new Bill of Rights." Especially did the Southern States need to win "their freedom from economic imperialism" and thereby transform the nation's economic problem number one "into a basic hope for the whole nation." "An economic, social, and cultural lag in any part of the country is an economic, social and cultural damage to all parts of the country." Following the War, after the victory of the democracies, human destiny will be "toward freedom, equality of opportunity, and the gradual fulfillment for all peoples of the noblest aspirations of the brothers of men . . . in the world neighborhood of human brotherhood." The United Nations offered a means of implementing these noble aspirations. "America must not again fail to join an association of nations for the organization and enforcement of peace."

By the first of May, 1944, the Memorial Fund Enlargement Campaign had received a total of $204,546.88. The end of World War II was still more than a year off, and structural steel and building materials were rationed and unavailable. The question that faced the Board in 1944 concerned the best use to which the money could be put. Should it be safely deposited in the bank or should it be invested? Governor Gardner had earlier promised that every dollar collected would be "preserved and safeguarded in every possible way," and this no doubt was still the *desideratum*. But at a special meeting on December 29, the Executive Committee of the Trustees authorized Governor Gardner to invest $75,000 "in such stocks or bonds that, in his judgment, would be reasonably safe and wise." December 29 proved to be a *dies faustus*; the stocks and bonds he purchased were both "safe and wise"; for on January 3, 1946, slightly more than a year later, Governor Gardner reported that $23,156.28 was received as profit from the sale of first mortgage railroad bonds sold in 1945, and $14,166.78 was received from interest and dividends on bonds and stocks.

Governor Gardner also was eager that the College acquire the more than 1000 acres of farm and timber land that the Cliffside Mills owned along the First Broad River. The land, lying only a mile and a half from the College, contained timber from which the needed lumber for the projected building program and the future expansion of the College would come. The property too contained a large quantity of building stone. The Board was getting ready to build; it simply awaited the end of the War. Although Governor Gardner did not wish it to be generally known, he determined to give the land to the College upon the authorization of the Executive Committee of the Board of Trustees that he buy it—an authorization which, quite likely, did not demand a lot of wire-pulling, behind-the-scenes conferences in smoke-filled corridors, or vigorous, cogent, and persuasive oratory. The Cliffside Mills agreed to sell, and Governor Gardner paid $35,000 for the 1058-acre farm.

The farm now became tied in with the vocational curricula that were looming large in the thinking of both the President and the Trustees. In the summer of 1945 the announcement was made to the Alumni Association that "the newly acquired property will be used to teach forestry to the students, establish a wood-working department at the College, provide lumber for the post-War building program, and pasture for a herd of dairy cattle." Earlier, on May 15, President Elliott told the Executive Committee of the Trustees of his "desire to secure a teacher to be called the Vocational Coordinator to instruct and carry out the work of the vocational subjects to be instituted at the College as a part of its regular training," and the President was instructed "to secure such a teacher as soon as possible." Gardner-Webb College, it should be pointed out, was to become no mere trade school. This President Elliott in his Report to the Board of Trustees, February 2,

1945, made clear: "We are . . . planning terminal work for those who wish to follow some trade but want more than a mere trade school can give them." Actually, according to President Elliott's article in the *Biblical Recorder*, June 13, 1945, Gardner-Webb College was proposing a daring and unique program. "We have in mind," the article said, "an educational venture that counts in its teaching . . . every agency of our area: farm, factory, shop, home, and church. The College is one element in a comprehensive plan for physical, economic, intellectual, and spiritual expansion." Instruction in the sciences and the humanities would be designed not only for those taking pre-professional courses, but as a background for all vocational work. The College, however, was to have vocational curricula in home economics, business education, farming, forestry, stock raising, repair of farm tools and automotive machinery, woodworking, electricity, radio, and perhaps photography and some instruction in textiles. These curricula were to be designed (1) to produce everything the College needed, (2) to make every activity a vital part of the instructional program, (3) to make the vocational curricula contribute by example, extension instruction, conferences, night courses, and co-operation with county, state, and federal agencies, to the economic development of the area, (4) to make it possible through these vocational curricula for every boy and girl in this area to make his way through the College, and (5) to train these boys and girls to go back home to develop their own communities.

By late summer 1945, much of the ardor for vocational training had cooled. In late August, President Elliott told the Shelby Rotary Club, "Gardner-Webb Junior College is fast coming to the place where it must decide whether its emphasis is to be principally upon cultural or vocational development, or both." By early the next month, the decision, so it seems, had been made. Chairman A. W. McMurry of the Executive Committee of the Board of Trustees announced that, after thorough consideration, a decision had been reached "not to extend the establishment of further courses in vocational education." Perhaps it was the cessation of hostilities that led to the decision; now, with the War over, plenty of students could be had who would want the traditional liberal arts courses. A better guess, however, would be that the Trustees were brought face to face with the staggering cost of equipment needed to offer the projected vocational curricula, that they swallowed hard once or twice from the initial shock, and that their curbing order was not then long in coming. This did not mean that President Elliott's dream of a college with a community-service concept had gone by the board. That dream was to be realized in other and more enduring and more practical ways.

In the spring of 1945, largely through the efforts of Lee B. Weathers, publisher of the Shelby *Star*, a valuable gift of books from the personal library of the famous novelist Thomas Dixon, Jr., and several of the original oil-painted illustrations for his novels were given to the College. This is the collection which appropriately is now housed in the Cleveland Room of the Dover Memorial Library. Thomas Dixon, Jr., is, by far, the most famous literary personage Cleveland County has produced. Along with a portion of his library, Dixon, now poverty-stricken and with less than a year to live, gave the College a typed carbon copy of his to-this-day unpublished autobiography —a revealing work of a happy-go-lucky, dyed-in-the-wool Southerner, who made more than a million dollars from his writings, made it but never tried to keep it.

Thomas Dixon's is an Horatio Alger, rags-to-riches story. He was born in Cleveland County in the midst of privation and poverty just before the end of the Civil War. But he became not only one of the most successful novelists of the early twentieth century, earning well over a million dollars with his pen, but he also wrote the screen play for *The Birth of a Nation*, the first tremendous screen success. Yet because of unwise investments—for

example $25,000 for the patent on a non-refillable bottle—
he died in poverty and was buried at the expense of his
friends, an end quite unlike that of an Horatio Alger hero.
Dixon knew his story was an interesting one; and before
his death in 1946, he prepared his autobiography which
he dedicated to "the large flock of black sheep known as
ministers' sons—by one of them."
Tom's difficulties began early. When he was only ten
years of age, his Grandma Dixon had him stop on his
way from school at Aaron Mooney's barroom, not far from
his Cleveland County, North Carolina, home and buy her
a bottle of bourbon. Tom's father, a Baptist minister and
a chaplain to the Ku-Klux Klan, found out about the purchase and soundly thrashed the boy. When Grandma
Dixon heard of the whipping, she got her things together,
and in a huff left the Dixon home. Although she was
eighty-seven at the time, she trudged on foot the eighteen
miles of bad road from the Dixon home to the home of a
relative in Kings Mountain, N. C. She lived to be one
hundred and four and sat on the platform at the centennial
celebration of the Battle of Kings Mountain.
Tom had a good deal of Grandma in him. When things
did not go to suit him, he turned in another direction.
Because he was six feet, three and a half inches tall and
weighed only one hundred and fifty pounds, he failed to
get a part in a New York play. On his way home to
Shelby, N. C., from New York, he decided to be a lawyer.
Later, at the suggestion of his father, he ran for the North
Carolina legislature and was elected before he was twenty-
one years old.
He later, however, gave up both law and politics and
entered the ministry. It was while he was pastor of the
Dudley Street Church in the Roxbury section of Boston,
Masschusetts, in the late 1880's, that something happened
which determined what he called his life's work. At a mass
meeting in Tremont Temple, Dixon listened to a man
make a speech on the "Southern Problem," which, as he
says in his unpublished autobiography, "sent a shock down

my spine that lifted me from my seat." The speaker had just returned from a tour of the South, where he had spent six weeks in "an exhaustive study of Southern life from car windows." The speaker declared that "the rebel flag still floats over every Southern town and village. The only way to save this nation from hell today is for Northern mothers to rear more children than Southern mothers!"

Dixon, on the front row, sprang to his feet and shouted with laughter.

"Who are you, sir?" thundered the speaker.

"A Southern white man who had lived in the South twenty-three years since the War and never saw a Confederate flag . . .," Dixon shouted back.

As he put it, "I made up my mind that night to write a triology on the South after the model of Henry Sienkiewicz's novels of Poland, WITH FIRE AND SWORD, THE DELUGE, AND PAN MICHAEL." He was determined to destroy sectionalism and reunite the nation.

In August of 1889, Dixon moved from Boston to New York to become pastor of the Twenty-Third Street Church. He resigned the pastorate of the Twenty-Third Street Church on March 10, 1895, and the next month opened the non-denominational People's Church. Less than four years later he resigned as pastor of the People's Church, determining to support himself by lecturing and to devote himself to writing the novels he long had planned to write.

Dixon, already famous as a lecturer, took twenty weeks of lecturing on a guarantee of $10,000. As he traveled from place to place, he worked on his first novel. Into his novel, THE LEOPARD SPOTS, so the author said, "had gone more than ten years of reading and preparation and this period of work had been preceded by a quarter of a century of living its scenes." The book was a sequel to UNCLE TOM'S CABIN, with the cruel Simon Legree transformed into a carpetbagger.

From Dixonville, Virginia, Dixon mailed the manuscript to Walter Hines Page of Doubleday, Page and Company.

Within forty-eight hours, Page sent a telegram of congratulation.

The book was a best seller from the beginning, and sales reached a hundred thousand copies before the first semi-annual report of royalties reached Dixon. The reviews were generous, and Dixon felt he "had given a tortured South a hearing in the forum of the world."

For the second of the triology—THE CLANSMAN—Dixon "dug through more than five thousand pamphlets and books in preparing the notes," and he wrote the novel in thirty days, working sixteen hours a day. It contained, according to its author, the first full-length portrait of Thad Stevens that had even been written and proved a greater sensation as a book than had THE LEOPARD'S SPOTS. The novel developed the story of the Ku-Klux Klan conspiracy, which overturned the Reconstruction regime in the South. It sold a million copies.

"The success of the book," Dixon said, "brought my thoughts back to the lode star on which they had been fixed from my first journey to New York." THE CLANSMAN must be dramatized and made a living thing in the theatre. The printed page would be read by five million people. The play, if successful, would reach ten million and with an emotional power ten times as great as in cold type. The play was a success and made $50,000 on its try-out run.

From his first three novels and the play based on THE CLANSMAN, Dixon made a comfortable fortune. But as he put it, he "heard the call of the Goddess of chance and became a small-fry Wall Street gambler." He invested $350,000 in stocks, mostly in United States Steel, but in the panic of 1907, he lost every dollar, and in one night his hair turned gray. Dixon was down, but he never knew what it meant to be out.

Dixon is primarily known today as the author of the screen play, *The Birth of a Nation*, the first million dollar movie. *The Birth of a Nation* was based on THE CLANSMAN. In vain Dixon offered his screen play to the major

producers, but finally a new company headed by H. E.
Aitken took the play, put it in the hands of D. W. Grif-
fith; and after two years and many disappointments, the
movie was finished. It was a phenomenal success. In ten
years it was seen by a hundred million people and grossed
$18,000,000.

In certain sections the picture—a private showing of
which President Woodrow Wilson, a Johns Hopkins friend
of Dixon's, saw in the East Room of the White House—
created a regular furor. A powerful group in Boston tried
to suppress the film, but the Mayor of Boston backed the
movie and the censor board endorsed it. In Chicago an
injunction was necessary in order that the film might be
shown unmolested there.

In twenty-five years, Dixon wrote twenty novels, nine
plays, and five motion pictures out of which he made
$1,250,000. He once held the deed to a beautiful island
off the North Carolina coast in Currituck Sound, which
took him all day to walk around. The craze of the land
boom caught him and he bought stock in a land company
in Florida. While roaming the hills of North Carolina, he
was persuaded to buy a mountain and "to build on it a
summer refuge for tired authors, musicians, actors, sing-
ers, and teachers." A company was formed to carry out
the venture known as WILDACRES, on a peak under the
shadow of Mount Mitchell. But the land boom collapsed
in 1929, and Dixon again lost every dollar he had.

Dixon, though, was philosophical about such matters.
"In my relation to material property," he said, "there has
always been a screw loose in my make-up. I've always been
able to make money but never tried to hold it. When times
got hard I've always been able to say to myself: 'Cheer up,
old boy, you'll soon be dead!' And what of it? If I should
die tomorrow, with my last breath I'd say: 'My love to
the world. I have lived a great, beautiful, thrilling adventure called life.' " And die he did on April 2, 1946.

On the third of January, 1946, three months before his
death, two letters—one from Mrs. Thomas Dixon, Jr.,

and one from Lee B. Weathers—were presented to the Executive Committee of the Board of Trustees "regarding a proper place for burial for Mr. Dixon." The Committee considered the very unusual item of business and agreed that the appropriate place would not be on the Gardner-Webb campus, but rather would be in the Sunset Cemetery in Shelby, where later he was buried on April 4, 1946.

Things continued to hum. The College was now laying the ground work surely and securely for real and substantial progress. W. Lawson Allen, Religious Director and Field Secretary, was, so the Trustees were told, doing "immeasurable good by creating interest in the College in churches" which had not been supporting the College; and Leonard Allen, brother of the Field Secretary, was appointed Business Manager. To encourage the teachers to do advanced study during the summers, the Trustees agreed to give them an honorarium of $25 for six weeks' work or $50 for twelve weeks' work. Mrs. J. D. Huggins, Sr., was made hostess to the girls with the responsibility of superintending the dormitory housekeeping. In the spring of 1945, President Elliott informed the Executive Committee of the Trustees that, if the Army would release Major I. N. Carr, who extended the greetings from the Army and Navy Training Forces at the inauguration of President Elliott, he hoped to secure him as Dean of the College. The Planning Committee met in Governor Gardner's home and recommended that the construction of certain buildings be begun in the near future. However, because of the spiraling cost of building materials and other expenses connected with building, the Executive Committee of the Trustees was, on August 3, 1945, told that "it would require $700,000 at the present time, under present costs," to "complete the $350,000 program as originally planned." The fund raising then must go on, must, if possible, increase the receipts of the Memorial Fund Enlargement Campaign to $400,000 or more by January 1, 1946. On August 29, 1945, the Executive Committee of the Trustees unanimously adopted a resolution that a dormitory be built to house at least forty-eight students and that this dormitory be completed for the 1946-1947 academic year "on the site selected by the Planning Committee in line with the J. E. Sirrine and Company Plan, Number Two." At the same time, the Committee voted to "defer the building of the Vocational Arts Building until we have ascertained further the advisability of it." With the passing of the vocational emphasis, the need for and thus the advisability of this building passed once and for all.

The Executive Committee of the Board of Trustees, at its meeting on August 29, 1945, also approved a motion by Governor Gardner that the architects be instructed to submit drawings for the Royster Health Clinic and for a central heating plant for the College—buildings which, along with the authorized dormitory, were to be ready, if possible, by the beginning of the academic year in September, 1946. The landscape gardener was to be requested also "to submit plans for carrying out the beautification of the campus as provided by Mr. Lester Hamrick." A little over a month later, on October 3, Business Manager Leonard Allen's duties were further increased by the Trustees. He now was instructed to "look after the forestry, agricultural, and dairying interest of the College," to "proceed now with selecting tenants for the cultivated land and houses" on the College farm, and to "secure a lumber man to cut . . . certain dead or near dead timber from this tract for lumber to be used at the College or put on the market" from the estimated 1,500,000 feet of standing saw timber on the 1058-acre farm.

In his Report on Christian Education, read to the Kings Mountain Association at its annual meeting in the fall of 1945, President Elliott called upon the churches to "go out in a great crusade to encourage boys and girls to go to college" and then to help provide the essentials of a good college "gladly as a token of our appreciation for the privilege of building a new world. The question is not can we afford to do it; it is can we afford not to do it." President Elliott defined Christian education as "a way of life that has love as its motive and human excellence as its goal . . . Christian education is the creation of high Christian character through the process of developing physical and mental skills." "Enforced self-discipline," President Elliott continued, "in the quest of skill and knowledge is the process; Christian character is the fruit." There was great value, he declared, to come to boys and girls who spent a "few years in an atmosphere of intellectual activity, honorable work, wholesome ideals, and high endeavor."

No New Year had ever brought with it before such scarcely dreamed of prospects for Gardner-Webb College as did 1946. On December 31, 1945, the total receipts of the Memorial Fund Enlargement Campaign were $481,-348.39, an average of $566 per day for the 850-day period since the Campaign began on September 1, 1943. And on the first day of January, the 851st day, $5,213 was added to the total. Governor Gardner, Chairman of the Finance Committee, was jubilant. His report and analysis of the Campaign declared that "this represents real evidence of the sustained faith and confidence of the friends of the College and alumni." Over 90 per cent of the funds had been contributed by citizens from Cleveland and Rutherford Counties; and not a dollar of the contributions had been spent for salaries or commissions, and only 1 per cent had been spent on printing, advertising, travel, literature, and typing. "If any community project," Governor Gardner said, "involving contributions of thousands of citizens, thousands of miles of travel, advertising and circulation of literature has ever been conducted for less cost, we have not heard of it." The Governor then reviewed the progress of the College since the beginning of the Campaign. The College campus on the 853rd day of the Campaign (Governor Gardner's report was dated January 3, 1946) consisted of 65 acres as compared with its less than 20 acres on September 1, 1943. The College too was free from debt, and the appraised value of all assets of the Col-

lege was $850,000 on this 853rd day. In 1944, "largely
through the continued and efficient efforts of B. G. Beason
and Guy H. Roberts," a nine-room duplex apartment was
constructed on the campus and was occupied by faculty
members in 1945. The late John F. Schenck had left the
College a valuable contingent gift of stock in the Lily
Mills Company of Shelby. Governor Gardner even mentioned the welcomed gift of a second-hand Chevrolet
truck and the gifts of meats, food, canned goods, and
"other innumerable small items." In Governor Gardner's
opinion, "one of the finest gifts to the College in 1945 was
made by S. W. Morrisett of Winston-Salem in a magnificent pipe organ at a cost of around $12,000," which was
to be installed some time in 1946 in the E. B. Hamrick
Memorial Building. "The gifts," Governor Gardner's report declared, "reveal the continuing tendency to bring
the College close to the hearts of our people."

But Governor Gardner did not want to leave the im-
pression that the College stood in need of nothing and that
all was well. To be sure, what seemed a great deal of money
was safely stashed away in the bank. But the buildings
were still on the drawing board. The most imperative need
just then was suitable housing for the College faculty. According to Governor Gardner, faculty housing was deplor-
able, and there could be "no finer test of the fidelity of
the faculty than exhibited by their patience and high service to the College under the most trying circumstances."
The report announced the projected John R. Dover Memorial Library, a library which would be the "best college
library of any junior college in North Carolina." The most
significant part of the report, however, was a recommendation that a committee be appointed "to study for consideration of the Executive Committee of the Board of
Trustees and the Kings Mountain and Sandy Run Associations the wisdom or unwisdom of Gardner-Webb [sic]
making application to enter into the denominational fold
of higher education with Wake Forest, Meredith, Mars

Hill, and Campbell College, with a view of rendering a more unified service to the cause of Christian education." The committee—composed of President Elliott, Chairman, Mrs. Rush Stroup, Dr. Zeno Wall, the Reverend John W. Suttle, the Reverend W. E. Pettit, the Reverend Tom Lawrence, Horace Easom, and Mal A. Spangler, Sr.—was appointed. In announcing the appointments to the newspapers, Chairman A. W. McMurry of the Executive Committee of the Board of Trustees said, "I think this matter is of great importance to the future of Gardner-Webb College, and I am sure this committee will look into the whole matter from every standpoint and be prepared to give friends of the College its best judgments." When the committee's report was ready, Chairman McMurry promised to call the Executive Committee together to receive it.

President Elliott, on August 12, 1946, reported. The committee of which he was Chairman declared its position: the College must "either raise an endowment to support the College or get into the State Convention to have advantage of its support or go broke in the lean years." President Elliott told the Executive Committee: "I assume that our chief interest in the matter is to build a college. Let me remind you that we have made practically no expansion since I have been here except in numbers of students and quality of instruction. . . . The time has come when we should expand and when we should increase the salaries of our teachers to the point where we can secure and hold good teachers." Professor Elliott warned, however, that "if Gardner-Webb should become a member of the [Baptist] Family of Colleges, it would be necessary for her to surrender some of her liberty for the privilege of a greater service. It would mean that we work out in cooperation with the Education Commission a greater program rather than trying to walk in glorious isolation alone; however, we would surrender none of our essential liberty." At the time of President Elliott's report, Gardner-Webb College was receiving only about $16,000 annually from 55 of the 108 churches in the two sponsoring Associations. From the State Convention it would receive $35,000 for current support under the proposed system of distribution. But to secure support from the State Convention would mean the relinquishing of at least two privileges the College then held: (1) The Charter of the College would have to be changed so as to provide for the election of Trustees as the Trustees of all Baptist institutions were elected, and (2) the College would have to cease to solicit gifts for current support from the churches.

The Executive Committee instructed President Elliott to meet with the Education Commission of the North Carolina Baptist State Convention to ascertain exactly what conditions Gardner-Webb College must meet and what advantages would come to the College from membership in the Convention. The requirements and advantages of membership were then to be presented to the Sandy Run and Kings Mountain Associations at their October meetings. President Elliott's findings were presented in the form of a resolution, which the Associations approved—a resolution "to accept the invitation of the Education Commission of the State Convention." The Associations, in turn, "fully authorized and empowered" the Board of Trustees of the College "to accept and complete such cooperative arrangement with the Baptist State Convention, and [to] cause the Charter of Gardner-Webb College to be so changed as to meet the requirements of the Constitution of the Baptist State Convention, and [to] file the Charter with the Secretary of State." The Associations, however, were warned that there were certain conditions attached to the acceptance of the proposal. Gardner-Webb College and its friends and supporters would be expected to give assurances that they would "produce a plant sufficient in quality and equipment to care for a student body of 400, thereby offering the facilities of a standard junior college," and that they would "guarantee an endowment sufficient to maintain such a plant." To provide such an endowment, the College had to have the income from $250,000 at 4 per cent, or $10,000 annually over and above other income, to maintain the College plant, but certain friends of the College had personally underwritten the requisite $10,000 until the Associations should have time to raise the $250,000 endowment. The Associations authorized the Trustees of the College to undertake the $250,000 campaign at their discretion, the only restriction being that the campaign should run no more than two years. About a month later, November 15, 1946, the Finance Committee of the Board of Trustees agreed to cease raising money for the Memorial Fund Enlargement Campaign for two years and to endeavor to raise at least $125,-000 in 1947 and a like amount in 1948 so that the College might "go to the meeting of the State Convention in the fall of 1948 with the money in hand."

It remained now only for the Baptist State Convention, later to meet at Asheville, N. C., to admit Gardner-Webb College conditionally into the Baptist family of colleges— a simple formality without any foreseeable opposition since the Council on Christian Education of the Convention had already endorsed the proposal and had initiated plans to begin its support of the College on January 1, 1947. The College's Charter had been amended to conform to the Constitution of the North Carolina State Baptist Convention; and on November 21, 1946, the responsibility for operating the College passed from the two sponsoring Associations to the Convention, which would thereafter allot a portion of its educational funds to the support of the College and would approve its Trustees. The property— the buildings, equipment, and campus—would continue to be owned jointly by the Kings Mountain and Sandy Run Associations.

The year 1946 was indeed an *Annus Mirabilus*. In his 1946 Report on Christian Education to the Associations, President Elliott disclosed that an earlier contribution of $75,000 by Jack and Charles Dover of Shelby for the erection of the John R. Dover Memorial Library had now, October 24, 1946, been increased to $100,000 by the

Dovers. On October 29, an announcement was made by the Cleveland Cloth Mills, a subsidiary of J. P. Stevens Company, that it was giving $50,000 to the College toward the erection of the James Webb Gardner Gymnasium on the campus, a gift "in recognition of the efficiency, ability, and generosity of James Webb (Decker) Gardner, who was General Manager of the Cleveland Cloth Mills at the time of his death, and as a tribute to his loyalty and devotion to the community and his understanding of human relations." Governor Gardner described the Stevens' gift as "most appropriate because the College Trustees, for lack of funds, had made no provision for the present construction of a much-needed gymnasium since demands for dormitory space and the high cost of building would more than absorb the $500,000 that had been raised for the building fund.

Earlier in the year, the College had been allotted 15 family-sized housing units by the National Director of the Federal Public Housing Authority at Atlanta, Georgia. This was a far cry from the 25 family units and 200 dormitory units the College had applied for under the Lanham Act, but the 15 units would help to meet partially the College's needs for veteran housing. On the third of May, Judge E. Yates Webb had turned the first spade of dirt for a dormitory, thus launching the building program for which the half million dollars had been raised. By the middle of October, the building fund had been increased to $575,000; but plans were now being made which would direct the money-raising attention of Horace Easom and Mal A. Spangler, Sr., to the necessary $250,000 endowment fund upon which the College's acceptance into the Baptist family of colleges was conditioned. Governor Gardner was sanguine that the necessary endowment would be raised promptly. Then, he said, "for the first time in its history, the permanent future of Gardner-Webb College will be reasonably insured when the College is admitted into full membership on terms of parity and equality with Wake Forest, Meredith, Campbell, and Mars Hill

Colleges. I have never believed that the College could continue to stand alone isolated from full participation in the fraternity of Baptist-supported colleges in North Carolina." How much he was interested in the future of Gardner-Webb College is reflected in the $75,000 contribution he made to the endowment fund. Jack and Charles Dover gave $50,000. Thus from three donors, half of the requisite endowment came.

President Harry S. Truman, about this time, appointed Governor Gardner as American Ambassador to the Court of St. James, and in a month or so he was to sail to his new post. Here was something new. Ambassador Gardner had done a lot of varied and difficult things from hoeing corn to consolidating North Carolina State College, the University at Chapel Hill, and Woman's College into the Greater University of North Carolina to running the United States Treasury, but this was to be the first time he had tried his hand at diplomacy. Ambassador Gardner was appointed early in January, 1947, to succeed W. Averell Harriman, who left London to become Secretary of Commerce. Ambassador Gardner—son of Oliver Harry Gardner, a country doctor, and the youngest of twelve children—had for some time been a pillar of strength in the Truman Administration. Ambassador Gardner's friend Drew Pearson said of him: "He knew how to salve individual hurts and convert them into cumulating aids. His suavity of manner—as of the Old South to which Gardner belonged by inheritance and practice—was an open sesame to the inner courts of society and the primordial haunts of those who sought to guide the fate of the nation." When Harry Hopkins was having trouble getting confirmed as Secretary of Commerce, it was O. Max Gardner who sat with him far into the night preparing him for the senatorial cross-examination. And when Stuart Symington was having his troubles as War Surplus Property Administrator, it was O. Max Gardner who gave him needed counsel.
A short time before accepting the diplomatic appoint-

ment, O. Max Gardner sold his rayon mill. He showed one friend the deposit slip in seven figures, and said, "You're looking at a real live millionaire, and I've no idea what to do with the money." But even in making money, O. Max Gardner never forgot human values nor the welfare of his fellowmen. His mill was the first in the South to adopt the minimum wage. Looking out for the other fellow, he found, paid dividends. Now with his mill sold and the money deposited, Ambassador Gardner hoped to devote the next years of his life to rendering on an international scale the same type of unselfish service that had characterized his interest in Gardner-Webb College.

This was not to be Ambassador Gardner's first visit to England, although his first trip forty-two years before had not been made in the luxury liner USS America. He crossed the Atlantic that time on a cattle boat as nursemaid to 500 seasick steers. His friend Bob Reynolds, later United States Senator from North Carolina, recruited Max as a cattle hand. Young Gardner arrived in London on the day the British were holding memorial services for the late United States Ambassador John Hay. He hailed a hansom cab to St. Paul's Cathedral, where the ceremony was to take place. The cab driver asked him who this John Hay might be. O. Max could have explained that he was a former United States Secretary of State and former Ambassador to Great Britain. Instead he said, "Hay is the man who wrote 'Little Breeches.'" Then the future Ambassador recited from memory Hay's famous poem of an Indiana youngster who got lost in a snowstorm when his team stampeded but who was finally found asleep in a haymow.

After his appointment to the Court of St. James, all sorts of people bobbed up with invitations to all sorts of social affairs; but Ambassador Gardner figured all this was a part of the new diplomatic game, and he went through with it. At one of these parties, given by Mrs. George Mesta and attended by Washington's most lorgnetted social set, flowery speeches flowed in rhapsodic language. Ex-

Senator Ashurst of Arizona even recited the list of United
States Ambassadors who later became Presidents of the
United States. Max Gardner, he implied, would be another.
Finally Max Gardner arose and told that diamond-be-
decked group of his first trip to England *on a cattle boat.*
He then recited "Little Breeches"; and even that starchy
audience applauded the man who quite likely got the no-
tion across to them that he intended to mix with the common man, rather than to spend his time "loafing around
the throne."

But on February 6, 1947, a few hours before he was
scheduled to sail for England, he died of coronary throm-
bosis at the Hotel St. Regis in New York. The first announcement of his death was made by the White House.
Presidential Secretary Charles G. Ross said President Truman was "deeply grieved and shocked." Few people outside of his family knew that, for many years, Max Gardner
had nursed a heart condition. It was his heart condition
that kept him from running for the Senate in 1944. He
was thoroughly disgusted with the wartime isolationism
of his cattleboat crony, Bob Reynolds, whose term was up
that year; but rather than run at the peril of his health,
he stepped aside in favor of his brother-in-law, Clyde R.
Hoey, who won an easy victory. His friend Drew Pearson
wrote: "But in the quiet hours of his last day upon American soil, . . . death came with a furtive tread, and as dawn
spread her roseate mantle over Gotham's canyoned streets,
the confident Carolinian sank into lasting rest."

Shelby, Cleveland County, and Gardner-Webb College
most keenly felt the loss of Ambassador Gardner. However, his friends who wished to honor his memory by sending flowers were asked by the Gardner family instead to
make contributions to Gardner-Webb College in lieu of
flowers for the funeral. Five days after Ambassador Gardner's death, the Flower Fund had soared to $2,375. Gard-
ner-Webb's faculty, students, and staff had given $999.06,
$500 of which had been contributed by Dr. W. Wyan
Washburn, the College's physician. By March 10, the

Gardner Flower Fund totaled $6,064. A few days later, the colored people of Shelby gave $200 to the Fund as an expression of their esteem for the late Ambassador. A spokesman for the group said that the gift came "from the colored people of Shelby in token of their love and esteem for that great American who was truly our friend and benefactor." Mrs. Gardner was very appreciative for what she called "a lovely expression by the colored people who were Max's friends."

On March 7, one month and one day after Ambassador Gardner's death, O. Max Gardner, Jr., told the Executive Committee of the Board of Trustees: "Ralph, Mother, and I plan to make a contribution through the Gardner Foundation of approximately $100,000 as a memorial to Daddy. We are not positive as yet as to the exact type of building or memorial we wish to make, but at present we are leaning toward the service type of building, perhaps a students' building." To help the Gardner family with its decision, President Elliott conducted a poll of the students. They felt that the greatest need was a student union building. The architects too felt that a student union building should be the next building erected. At the next meeting of the Executive Committee on March 29, O. Max Gardner, Jr., disclosed that the Gardner Foundation was the recipient of a $100,000 life insurance policy, "which we feel my father would have wished used to improve the physical plant of the College." Max, Jr., then made the following proposition to the Executive Committee:

That you authorize the Board of Directors of the Gardner Foundation to secure architects to make detailed drawings and secure bids for the construction; and for the Directors of the Foundation to accept or reject these bids as they see fit; and if possible to start construction of the $100,000 Max Gardner Student and Activities Building. The architects have estimated the cost of this building to be between $70,000 and $90,000. We want to say that if the building should cost $110,000, including furnishings, we will still build it—[just] as if it costs $70,000, we will build it; and if it costs $125,000, we will build it and equip it; . . . the Directors of the Foundation will build it and be responsible for it. I will be out of State College by June and I will be free for approximately the next 6 months to look after it; and if this Committee accepts this proposition, we would like authority to employ the firm of Van Wageningen and Cothran. The Foundation will assume all cost.

The Reverend John W. Suttle made the motion that the Committee accept the proposition. Chairman Hill Hudson turned and said to Max, Jr.: "It touches us all—it does me. I know this body is in full agreement with the wishes of the Gardner family. Max, you can express to your family just how we feel toward this plan. It touches me because I loved your Daddy, and to have you spend 6 months of your time—that will be a service we could never procure from anyone else; and if you are here, you will look after the small dormitories. This service to be rendered by Max we could not hope to get from any other source in the world."

This was the year—1947—that the building of the modern campus was pushed forward. The minutes of the Executive Committee for May 30, 1947, contain this significant statement: "We sincerely believe that at this time the first plan of action, to build NOW, is most important and imperative. We have based this decision on the opinions of others and of ourselves, and have reached our conclusion in the light of our whole building program." This statement was contained in a report signed by O. Max Gardner, Jr., John R. Dover, and Guy H. Roberts. The decision of these men was based upon their faith in the future of Gardner-Webb College. "We realize," they reported, "the impossibility of building a great college in one man's lifetime. We can only look upon the accomplishments of the past four to five years as a rule and guide for the next fifty years. We know that our efforts are only the beginnings: we cannot be the Alpha and Omega. We believe that the future of Gardner-Webb is a glorious one and that Almighty God will provide new friends and new funds as we progressively improve our facilities for offering the best in Christian education."

There seems to have been all along some dissatisfaction with the J. S. Sirrine plan for the College. Before his death, Governor Gardner and members of the Planning Committee studied some plans submitted by Van Wageningen and Cothran, members of the American Institute of Architects and architects experienced in college architectural design and planning. Governor Gardner and the Planning Committee were impressed. They consequently made a thorough study of the needs of the College, its facilities at the time, and recommended a new building program for the College, plans for which the architects had ready by the end of April 1947. On July 15, contracts were let for two new dormitory sections of the Girls' Dormitory. These units, which were to be added to the already completed $75,000 central unit, were parts of the Van Wageningen and Cothran master plan. The three units, when completed, would house 98 girls. The contract for the two wings had to be relet when Contractor C. P. Neal elected not to accept the contract awarded him earlier. However, by September the contract had been awarded to Robert H. Pinnix, Gastonia contractor, and actual construction had started.

Even before construction on the John R. Dover Memorial Library was begun, two new special collections of books for the library were secured. One was to be known as the "J. L. Jenkins Memorial Library for Rural Pastors." This special collection was a tribute to a man who, at that time, had already devoted more than thirty years to preaching and teaching. The Jenkins Memorial Library was started by a spontaneous gift from a Washington, D. C., resident who had sat under Mr. Jenkins when he was the unpaid President of Boiling Springs Junior College. Others made donations for books for the special collection, and some ministers promised to donate books "for the aid of the thousands of young ministers who eventually will study at Gardner-Webb." When Mr. Jenkins began instructing young preachers in homiletics and Scriptural interpretation, his classroom was wherever he happened to be—in his home, in the boys' rooms, or on a bench under a campus tree. Soon the size of the classes outgrew the out of doors, and the College added homiletics to its curriculum. This did not mean that the informal classes were discontinued. Rather, "The Doctor," as his preacher-student friends called him, maintained an open house for his "boys."

The other special collection was the library of the late A. C. Dixon, brother of the famous author of *The Birth of a Nation*, whose library the College had acquired earlier, and one of the most celebrated preachers of his day. It was given to the College by Mrs. Clara Dixon Richardson of Black Mountain, N. C., daughter of the Reverend Mr. Dixon. Mrs. Richardson, in her letter to President Elliott concerning the gift, said that she was happy that the College was interested in the books and that she felt it peculiarly appropriate for them to be housed in the College library since Cleveland County and its people had always been close to her father's heart. Mrs. Richardson expressed regret that she did not have her father's complete library—the complete library of the man who occupied the pulpit of such well-known churches as the Moody Tabernacle in Chicago and the Spurgeon Tabernacle of London. But, as she pointed out, when he went to London, he gave away many of his books; and when he retired from the active ministry, he bought a home at Ridgecrest, N. C., boxed his books and sent them there, but many were stolen. His once great library had been, at the time of the gift, reduced to some 500 volumes, which Mrs. Richardson had placed in the study of a church at Black Mountain for the use of the pastors there. "I feel," Mrs. Richardson wrote, however, "[that] they should be in the hands of students. . . . I have held onto these books with a certain amount of sentiment, but I shall feel much happier knowing that they can be used."

Nothing, however, could be allowed to make the Trus-

tees forget their commitment to raise $250,000 for endow-
ment; and Horace Easom was not one to let them forget.
Very early in the spring of 1947, Mr. Easom reasoned with
the Trustees that someone ought to be "secured to do the
detail work of contacting the church to secure approximately $187,000— . . . someone . . . who would contact
first the pastors of the churches, then the deacons, and
finally, when the groundwork has been laid, the churches
themselves." Here was Horace Easom's plan. He told the
Executive Committee that unless something was done and,
in his opinion, done *now* to secure the needed money, the
Trustees of the College and the two sponsoring Associations would have to tell the Baptist State Convention at
its meeting in the fall of 1948 that they had defaulted on
their promise.

The person Mr. Easom hoped to secure proved to be the
Reverend Ben Coleman Fisher. However, when he came
to Gardner-Webb in 1947 as Chairman of the English
Department "with some responsibilities in the field of public relations," surely no one, least of all Ben, had the faint-
est idea that the young minister would acquire, in a few
years, a wide reputation as a fund-raiser *par excellence*.
Ben Fisher was born on May 27, 1915, in the heart of the
Great Smoky Mountains at Webster, N. C. From the
Fruitland Institute at Hendersonville, N. C., he went to
Wake Forest College, graduating *cum laude* in 1938. The
next year he attended Andover-Newton Theological Seminary on a full scholarship, serving, while receiving his
theological training, as a pastor of a rural church in New
Hampshire. Mr. Fisher majored in rural church sociology
and wrote his thesis on "The Comparison of Northern and
Southern Protestantism as Seen in the Rural Church."
After receiving the B.D. degree, Mr. Fisher was pastor at
the First Baptist Church of Nashville, N. C., from 1941
to 1944. In 1944, he became pastor of the First Baptist
Church of Newton, N. C., from which he came in 1947
to Gardner-Webb College.

Horace Easom was shortly to relinquish his work with

the Gardner-Webb Endowment Fund Campaign. Even in the spring of 1947, it was rumored that Wake Forest College was trying to get Mr. Easom to direct a statewide financial campaign. Mr. Easom admitted he had "telephone calls and other contacts, but no propositions." But the proposition was destined to come; and on March 15, 1948, Ben Fisher was released "temporarily" from his teaching assignment to direct the Endowment Fund Campaign. Under Mr. Easom's leadership, $142,000 of the necessary $250,000 had been secured. Mr. Fisher's job then was simply to raise $108,000—a sizeable amount even for a man of his proportions.

But President Elliott and others were concerned not only with buildings and money-raising, but also with the academic standing and accreditation of the College. In his 1946 Annual Report to the Trustees, President Elliott declared that "it is of primary importance that we secure membership in the Southern Association of Colleges." On January 29, 1948, in a report to the Trustees, O. Max Gardner, Jr., traced the phenomenal development of the institution under the leadership of President Elliott in its plant; in its assets, which on November 18, 1947, had reached more than a million dollars; in its student body, which had jumped from 169 to 420 in five years; in its expanded curriculum and faculty; and in the high place which it had assumed among the Baptist colleges in North Carolina. "The next step upward to be sought," the report declared, "is membership in the Southern Association of Colleges." The two—membership in the Southern Association of Colleges and Secondary Schools and full membership in the North Carolina Baptist State Convention— were to be tied in together. It was a matter of being able to deal with two desirable birds with one quarter-of-a-million-dollar stone.

The immediate task then facing Ben Fisher was the raising of $108,000 in the little more than six short months remaining before the North Carolina Baptist State Convention met. Ben tightened his belt around his goodly girth. No gift was to be scorned. As the six months wore on, the situation became more pressing with each passing day. One afternoon, Ben went to see Dathia Elliott, successful farmer, businessman, Baptist layman, and civic leader, at his apple house a few miles from the College. Mr. Elliott had become actively interested in Gardner-Webb College some time before. Ben explained the desperate situation facing the College and asked him whether or not he could see his way clear to give at least $1000. He paused a moment and then said, "I'll see what I can do." About two days later, Ben received a phone call from Mr. Elliott, suggesting that they meet at the Sandwich Shop in Boiling Springs. The two met there and talked for a few minutes. Then Mr. Elliott, who had come directly from his cotton gin, reached into his coat pocket, took out a large roll of money, and slowly counted off fifty twenty-dollar bills, some of which had cotton lint stuck to them.

One of the most magnificent illustrations of the range of interest in Gardner-Webb's future was the action of the women of Zoar Church in near-by Shelby. The women wanted to give the College $1000 on the Endowment Fund Campaign. To get the money, they planted, tilled, and harvested an acre of cotton. Hill Hudson, Gardner-Webb Trustee and Shelby merchant, heard of the commendable project and gave the women $1000 for their bale of cotton.

The College had many other friends to whom Ben Fisher could turn. For instance, there was Belton G. Beason, who started his sandwich business in Boiling Springs during the depression with three roosters, from which he made chicken salad. From those first sandwiches, which he sold for a nickel, he built a large and profitable business. Outside of his family, he had three loves: his church, his community, and Gardner-Webb College. He contributed himself and, in addition, rode thousands of miles in his own automobile to solicit funds from corporations and individuals. About a year before his death, Mr. Beason suffered a severe heart attack. But he lost none of his interest in the College; and with his recovery, he wanted to continue his service to the institution. About a month before his last illness, he and Ben Fisher had planned to go to Charlotte to see some friends about some contributions. When Ben entered the Boiling Springs Drug Store, their appointed meeting place, he saw that Mr. Beason did not seem to be well, and he said, "Belton, are you sure you feel like making this trip today?" He looked up, hesitated a moment, and then said, "Ben, I don't think I have long. I don't know of any better way that I would like to spend the time that I have than in working for our College."

One of Gardner-Webb's most loyal and devoted friends through the years has been Rush Hamrick, Sr., for many years operator of a wholesale drug firm in Shelby. Through his business connections, Mr. Hamrick had a host of friends all over Western North Carolina and upper South Carolina. If he ever had any misgivings about hurting his own business by constant solicitation from his customers, he hid his fears. Some years back, a fire broke out in his warehouse and destroyed thousands of dollars worth of drugs and goods. Two days after the fire, Mr. Hamrick and Mr. Fisher had scheduled a trip to Gastonia and Charlotte. Mr. Fisher felt that his companion for the trip would not have the heart to be out raising money for Gardner-Webb College under the circumstances. But when the matter was mentioned to him and he was asked whether or not he would like to postpone the trip for a few days, he replied, "Humph, the College still needs the money."

Another tireless worker in fund-raising and the development of Gardner-Webb has been Claude Hinson, a Belmont, N. C., business man. Mr. Hinson was a key man in the endowment campaign, the campaign for the James Webb Gardner Dormitory for men, the campaign for the President's home, the farm development campaign, and the Church-Community Development campaign. In addition, he gave the College the faculty duplex apartment house which stands directly behind Decker Hall. On one occasion, when the College was attempting to raise some money for the student loan fund, he did a characteristic thing. The textile business was going through one of its periodic slumps, and money was coming slowly. A short time before, Mr. Hinson had lost, quite unexpectedly, his small son. When approached about a contribution, he dropped his head for a moment, stared at his desk, then threw his head back with a characteristic gesture and said to Mr. Fisher: "Ben, I'll tell you what I am going to do. We had an insurance policy on our little boy to help him in his college education. We are going to give that to Gardner-Webb to establish a loan fund to help students there."

Then, too, there were others. No woman in North Carolina has supported more consistently the cause of Christian education than has Mrs. Rush Stroup. She has been a tireless worker and a generous contributor in all of Gardner-Webb's campaigns. Jesse Bridges, now President of Shelby's Union Bank and Trust Company, was a key man in almost every campaign Mr. Fisher conducted. He was always willing to give a part of each day, if necessary, to solicitations. Holt MacPherson, editor of the Shelby *Star* for a number of years, was a close personal friend of Governor Gardner and a man with a deep and warm interest in Gardner-Webb College. Until the News Bureau was established at the College, Holt MacPherson practically served as a one-man public relations staff, serving, in addition, on various fund-raising committees and being responsible for several large gifts that the College received. Lewis Ludlum, who, at the time of the Endowment Fund Campaign, was Associational Missionary for the Kings Mountain Association, was one of the best friends and hardest workers that Gardner-Webb ever had. When Gardner-Webb was carrying on the Campaign in the churches with the permission of the Baptist State Convention, Mr. Ludlum put all the force of his office and his personal influence behind the fund-raising efforts. Helping in every fund-raising drive was Lee B. Weathers, publisher of the Shelby *Daily Star*, who had wide connections in the business world. He gave and influenced his friends to give. For a number of years, Carlos Young, Shelby business man, had shared a part of his company's profits with Gardner-Webb College. Himself a victim of an almost fatal illness when he was a young man, he had a deep sympathy for anyone struggling to get through college. He said to Mr. Fisher on one occasion, "Don't you ever let a boy or girl who really has the stuff drop out of school over there. You come to me. If we don't have it, we'll go find it." And while it is well known what the Gardners have done for the College, it perhaps is not generally known how much personal time Ralph Gardner gave to the financial drives of the College. On several occasions when the campaigns were bogging down, Ralph Gardner flew in from Washington to lend a hand. And what is true of Ralph Gardner is also true of Charles I. Dover—a man who not only contributed personally, but also gave endless hours of personal attention to the financial problems of the College. According to Mr. Fisher, "No man ever worked more sincerely or any harder than did Charlie Dover. He and his brother Jack were the mainstays in the financial campaigns."

With such a corps of ardent and sacrificial supporters—to which could be added W. Hill Hudson, Tom Cornwell, Paris Yelton, Guy Roberts, Clifford Hamrick, Mrs. J. D. Lineberger, Carson Stout, Herbert Bridges, Guy Carswell, Hill Hudson, Jr., Mrs. J. Warren Gamble, and a host of others—Ben Fisher's success in raising the $108,000 and his success in subsequent fund-raising drives were assured. As Mr. Fisher expressed it, "The secret of any successful fund-raising effort always lies in the willingness of individuals to assume personal responsibility for solicitation. No one man can more than scratch the surface in fund-raising. Gardner-Webb has been fortunate through the years in having many men who were willing not only to give but to go out and ask others for money." This is not to say, however, that the $108,000 came easy. Quite the contrary. But nonetheless it came. To accomplish the goal

two new ideas were tried. On March 7 at the meeting of
the College's Executive Committee of the Trustees, Clifford E. Hamrick raised the question as to whether or not
one hundred men who would give $1000 each could be
found in Rutherford, Cleveland, and Gaston Counties. He
suggested that possibly twenty-five or thirty men could
be contacted who would promise to contribute $1000 each.
They and others to make up the one hundred would then
be invited to a dinner at which an attempt would be made
to secure a pledge from each man present to give $1000
to the Endowment Fund Campaign. The suggestion was
received with a good deal of favor. By April 27, the number had been cut from one hundred to fifty; but the Thousand Club officers were busy. On October 10, thirty
participating persons and business concerns, representing
$37,000 in contributions, were present at the first meeting
of the Thousand Club at a dinner in the Huggins-Curtis
Building on the College campus. At the meeting, Ben
Fisher reported that the endowment drive was within
$20,000 of the $250,000 goal. The other idea was to establish what came to be known as the Living Endowment.
This plan recognized realistically the inability of many to
give $1000 outright who could, however, give steadily to
the endowment fund. Clifford Hamrick, President of the
Thousand Club, declared, "It has been my dream for a
number of years to see some plan enacted at Gardner-
Webb through which all the hundreds of alumni and
friends could make an annual contribution."

President Phil Elliott stated publicly that he had no in-
tention of going to the meeting of the North Carolina
Baptist State Convention in Charlotte in November unless
he could report to the Convention that Gardner-Webb
College had met the conditions for unqualified membership
in the Convention. However, President Elliott *did*, to be
sure, go to Charlotte and made the following report to
the Convention:

> According to the records of the Council on Christian Education,
> Gardner-Webb College was asked, as a prerequisite to becoming

a member of the Baptist family of colleges, to raise by the time of this Convention, one quarter of a million dollars for endowment in addition to three quarters of a million to be spent on the College plant.

I am authorized to announce that, by a margin, the College exceeded both requirements. All College assets are listed at cost. Gardner-Webb, therefore, asks for full recognition as a member institution of this Convention.

Following the report of its President, Gardner-Webb College was unconditionally received as a member of the Convention.

Gardner-Webb had now made one more significant step forward, but President Elliott was vitally concerned that it accomplish still another of his cherished goals. In the President's Report to the Board of Trustees, May 30, 1947, he reminded the Trustees of the College's attempt to meet the requirements of the Southern Association of Colleges and Secondary Schools. Already a committee—composed of Dr. M. C. Huntley, Executive Secretary of the Southern Association, J. B. Young of Mississippi, and Dr. W. S. Rogers of Georgia—had made a thorough survey of the College. To quote the President, "The committee found a few rough patches in the plant and program, but nothing that cannot be fairly easily overcome. The committee was most cordial and complimentary. Our plans and program they found in all basic essentials in line with the best educational thought. They assured us that there was little question of our going into the Association when the vote is taken; and they complimented the College on the rapidity and quality of its progress." On December 22, 1947, in another President's Report to the Trustees, President Elliott declared, "We are in sight of membership. We now meet, I believe, the minimum standards. If we show evidence of progress, I have great hope that we shall be admitted at the next meeting." During the 1948-1949 academic year, Gardner-Webb College was able to meet the rigid standards of the Southern Association and was admitted to membership at its annual meeting in Memphis, Tennessee, on December 2, 1948.

Earlier in the year, Treasurer of the College O. Max Gardner, Jr., in a report of the progress the College had made over a five-year period, made a significant declaration: "We sincerely believe at this time it is important and imperative to continue our building program. . . . We have a firm belief that such signs of progress as building of the athletic field, landscaping the campus, erection of the new dormitory for veterans, addition of the government units, quonset huts, and completion of the two new dormitory wings will be of inestimable value in maintaining a high interest in the College, but primarily in securing additional funds for continued building." The report further stated: "We have based our decision on our great faith in the future of Gardner-Webb. We can look only upon the accomplishments of the past as a rule and guide for the coming years. We believe that the future of Gardner-Webb is a glorious one and that Almighty God will provide new friends and funds as we progressively improve our facilities for offering the best in Christian education."

A little less than two months after this report, Mrs. O. Max Gardner, Sr., President of the Gardner Foundation, announced that, through the Foundation, the building of the O. Max Gardner Memorial Student Union would soon be begun. The firm of R. H. Pinnix, which at that time was completing the two student dormitories, was awarded the general contract. It was estimated, at the time, that the cost of the building and its complete furnishings and equipment would be approximately $150,-000. Designed by Van Wageningen and Cothran, the building was to be of Williamsburg architecture and was to have on the main floor a student lounge, society halls, and publication and student council rooms. On the ground floor was to be a cafeteria large enough to serve nearly 500 at one time, together with a kitchen, student exchange, and other facilities.

To express his gratitude for the gift of the building, President Elliott wrote the following letter to Mrs. Gardner:

Dear Mrs. Gardner:

I want to say to you and through you to your sons Ralph and Max, Jr., and to the other directors of the Gardner Foundation that the contemplated Student Union Building by the Gardner family in honor of your illustrious husband will meet one of the pressing needs of the College, both now and in the future. Food, rooming facilities, and curriculum are the three basic material essentials of any college. Food and its service is closely allied to the social life of an institution. The building, which you propose, will give complete opportunity for adequate and attractive serving of food. The student exchange, the lounge, and the dining hall will add immeasurably to the cultural life of the campus. The student will have, as a result of this building, the privilege of a finer social, mental, and spiritual association as the basic means of learning to live together.

The building will enrich the extracurricular activities further by means of the society halls, the offices for student publications, and the opportunity for social games. It will add to the curricular offerings by affording day students a place to study and to all a central means of carrying out the purposes of our guidance program. Also, through the guidance program, the publications, the Alumni Association, and the banquet hall, an effective public relations program can be advanced. (It is no longer true that Mark Hopkins' boy on one end of a log and a teacher on the other make a school. No school can exist in this day of competition without adequate buildings and equipment.) I should say without hesitation that this building will meet a pressing need of the College now.

May I take this opportunity, therefore, to congratulate and commend you for this great humanitarian idea of memorializing a great humanitarian. May I also express the undying gratitude of everyone connected with Gardner-Webb College, of everyone who loves boys and girls, and wants to see their future enriched and our way of life made secure.

With warm personal regards, I am

Sincerely yours,
(Signed) P. L. Elliott

United States Senator J. M. Broughton, junior Senator from North Carolina, had agreed to deliver the dedicatory address at the formal dedication of the O. Max Gardner Memorial Student Union on Easter Sunday, April 17, 1949. Senator Broughton died, however, before that Easter Sunday, and he was replaced by United States Senator Clyde R. Hoey, a brother-in-law of Ambassador Gardner and an associate with him in business and politics before the Ambassador's death. Approximately 3000 friends and former students of the College witnessed the ceremony which took place on the terrace of the new $155,000 building. The invocation was delivered by the Reverend J. L. Jenkins, pastor of the Boiling Springs Baptist Church. Ben C. Fisher, who in the fall of 1948 had been made Executive Assistant to the President of Gardner-Webb College, made a brief address of welcome. Senator Hoey's address followed. "O. Max Gardner was," he declared, "the greatest man that Cleveland County ever produced!" "It was," he continued, "as an educational statesman that Max Gardner reached his greatest heights." Senator Hoey then pointed to the consolidation of the three units of the Greater University of North Carolina during Max Gardner's term as Governor of North Carolina. "Following in the footsteps of Thomas Jefferson, another great Southern educational leader and statesman," Senator Hoey said, "Max Gardner had the vision and foresight to see the need of a great junior college; and consequently he turned his thought and well-directed efforts to the stabilization and rehabilitation of Gardner-Webb." Further Senator Hoey declared, "The history of this institution with its early struggle for existence as Boiling Springs Junior College and its rebirth when it became Gardner-Webb College reads like a romance." Senator Hoey then made reference to the decisive steps in Gardner-Webb's advance—the increase in facilities, the creation of an endowment fund, Gardner-Webb's acceptance into the North Carolina Baptist State Convention, and the benefits coming to the College under the protection and guidance of the Baptist denomination. "This student union building—the latest addition to the expansion program—which we dedicate today," he said, "will be a continual reminder of the spirit, the genius, the driving force and power of the one man more than any other who contributed to the regeneration of this institution."

The College too needed a President's home. Quite likely the women of the Kings Mountain and Sandy Run Associations felt this need more keenly than did the men. Mrs. W. P. Biggerstaff, President of the Kings Mountain Woman's Missionary Union, in a letter to the Associational W.M.U.'s, called attention to the apartment in which President Elliott and his family lived—a small apartment with only two bedrooms for the family of six. At their annual spring meeting at the Poplar Springs Church, the women of the Kings Mountain Woman's Missionary Union voted to renew their efforts to raise the remaining $1000 on a previous $2500 pledge and, in addition, to raise $1500 more for a President's home at Gardner-Webb College. The women of the Sandy Run Association were attempting to raise $1000 toward the home, which, it was estimated, would cost $20,000 to build but which, like most estimates, proved too low. The Board of Trustees, in cooperation with the Associational W.M.U.'s, appointed the following Committee on the President's Home: Mrs. Rush Stroup, Chairman, Mrs. J. R. Cline, Mrs. O. Max Gardner, Sr., B. G. Beason, Dr. Wyan Washburn, and President and Mrs. P. L. Elliott. The Committee recommended to the Board of Trustees that $8,000 from the Memorial Building Fund be used for this project, a recommendation unanimously passed, although the amount later had to be increased to $12,000. In 1947, the Woman's Missionary Unions of the Kings Mountain, Sandy Run, and Gaston Associations had on hand about $4000. The next year a campaign was launched to raise the rest of the funds needed to complete the home, which ultimately was valued at $30,000. According to Ben Fisher, Mrs. Rush Stroup "was the moving spirit behind the completion of the building." The Drexel Furniture Company of Drexel, N. C., sent one of its top interior decorators and designers to study the den. The result was custom-built, specially designed furniture for this part of the house. The kitchen equipment, valued at several thousand dollars, was furnished by Claude Hinson of Belmont, N. C.; and the dining room was furnished by the Lenoir Chair Company. Ed Harrell of Newton, N. C., donated the furnishings for the guest room. In all about $4000 worth of furniture and equipment was donated by friends of the College.

On the twelfth of November, 1948, the Board of Trustees of Gardner-Webb College unanimously approved the letting of a contract "in the immediate future for the construction of a dormitory for 100 boys at Gardner-Webb College." The College urgently needed this building. By crowding every available space in 1948-1949, the College had been able to accommodate 124 boys; fifty found quarters in the community, but many were turned away. Out of gratitude to the Gardner Foundation for its generous gift of $50,000, the Trustees voted unanimously to name the new dormitory for James Webb Gardner, affectionately known as "Decker." In addition to this, the J. P. Stevens Company graciously allowed its gift of $50,-000, which it had previously designated for a gymnasium as a memorial to James Webb Gardner, to be used instead to liquidate the debt on the dormitory. Constructed and furnished, the dormitory cost $236,619.42, of which, in addition to the $100,000 mentioned above, $75,000 came from the Memorial Fund and $61,619.42 came from business and professional men, industry, alumni, and friends of the College.

As early as the fall of 1946, Gardner-Webb College began sustained radio programming. In the fall of 1947 the Public Relations Department undertook to give a series of broadcasts weekly over stations WBBO in Forest City, N. C., and WOHS in Shelby, N. C. The College had no equipment of any kind, and the program director and students would go to the radio station an hour early for rehearsal. This led to one dramatic incident in Forest City when the Ford station wagon, in which eight students were riding, stalled on the railroad tracks during a sleet storm. It was only a matter of seconds after panicked passengers had emptied the station wagon that it was hit and completely demolished by a fast-moving passenger train. Largely as a result of this near disaster, the College began to look around for some means of originating broadcasts on the campus. The First Baptist Church of Maiden, N. C., gave a public address system, which was used to simulate and practice broadcasts. But it was Mrs. Paris Yelton, at the time a member of the Board of Trustees, and a graduate of old Boiling Springs High School, who made a substantial initial gift for the purchase of the console, turntables, and the microphone of what is now known as the Huggins Memorial Communications Center. As a result of the establishment of the Communications Center, a direct phone-line hookup was possible to radio station WOHS in Shelby.

Also in the fall of 1947, upon instructions from the Board of Trustees, the Department of Public Relations undertook to establish a News Bureau from which weekly releases would go to state and county papers. However, it was not until the fall of 1948, with the employment of Santford Martin, Jr., that the College was able to develop an outstanding News Bureau. Prominent among the releases from the News Bureau were special monthly features appearing in the large Sunday papers from Wilmington to Asheville. Included in these Sunday features were stories about the guidance program, the a capella choir, the radio center, the dedication of the Gardner Memorial Student Union, the campus spring fashion review, the erection of the Royster Memorial Building, and the extensive civic-banquets program of the College cafeteria. Such features were released to at least fifteen North Carolina newspapers, each with over 10,000 circulation. Supplementing regular news during the 1949-1950 academic year, the Bureau wrote the script for three major radio broadcasts over the southeastern FM network of station WMIT. The autumn program from the top of Mt. Mitchell, and the Christmas and Easter programs from the campus featured the College's a capella choir in special music and adapted script.

To paraphrase the first two lines of Wordsworth's

"Tintern Abbey," seven years had past; seven summers, with the length of seven long winters! and again the special committee which O. Max Gardner brought to study Gardner-Webb College and to recommend a course of action for the College reassembled to check on how well that program had been carried out and to suggest further progressive development for Gardner-Webb College. Of the original committee—which was composed of Dr. J. Henry Highsmith, Chancellor John W. Harrelson, Professor Claude Teague, Dr. Fred W. Morrison, and Dr. Thurman Kitchin—only Dr. Kitchin was unable to be present for the inspection of the physical facilities at Gardner-Webb and to aid in the qualitative, as well as quantitative, analysis of the College and its work. The Committee was more than delighted. According to Chancellor Harrelson of North Carolina State College, Gardner-Webb had advanced more in the seven years just past than most colleges advance in fifteen years. The Committee found the progress at Gardner-Webb to be "truly remarkable" and "the faith that the late O. Max Gardner had in his neighbors and friends of the institution" more than justified. "His dream," the Committee said, "is coming true. There is a real job for Gardner-Webb to do. The foundation has been laid for a real achievement and a high order of service." The committee also found the "well-trained young men who have been employed as teachers" another "noticeable feature" of the College. Concerning the faculty, the committee further said, "In a program of modern education, it is necessary to have dynamic teachers, men and women, to direct the activities of youth. Their enthusiasm and vision, together with the wisdom and experience of the more mature members of the faculty, make a fine team for dealing with young people." Praise too was not lacking "for the generosity and interest of Gardner-Webb supporters in the matter of financial backing." But all was not perfect, and the time had not yet arrived for the College to rest on its laurels. Indeed that time may never—indeed, should never—arrive. The advisory team, there-

fore, suggested the immediate construction of the new
men's dormitory, soon to be begun, the building of a new
central heating plant, the erection of the new Dover Memorial Library, and the construction of a new gymnasium.
They also placed strong emphasis on the College's "watching and adopting the most practical trends in vocational
education."

In his Report to the Trustees, May 30, 1947, President
Elliott included a recommendation from Dr. Wyan Washburn, College physician, "that the Trustees make a decision
in the near future as to whether the College wants simply
an infirmary for college students or wants a Community
Health Center, which would include facilities for an infirmary." For a year or more before Dr. Washburn's recommendation to the Trustees, President Elliott and Dr.
Washburn had been discussing, from time to time, the
possibility of a combination infirmary and health center.
Before Dr. Washburn's discharge from the United States
Army Medical Corps in August of 1946, Boiling Springs
had only one physician, the late Dr. J. Y. Hamrick, who
was in ill health and semi-retired. Miss Eunice Highsmith
was the College nurse, and the infirmary was in the old
Huggins-Curtis Building. It actually was an infirmary in
name only since there were no beds in the so-called infirmary and no facilities for overnight care. In 1946, Dr.
Washburn established an office for general practice of
medicine in Boiling Springs and accepted a position as
College physician. He moved into what was known as the
old Dr. Wood Drug Store building, the only building then
available in Boiling Springs, a structure he used as a resi-
dence, an office, a clinic, and an infirmary for the students.
But Dr. Washburn hoped for better things for both the
community and the College; he expressed his hopes to the
Trustees of Gardner-Webb College; and his hopes materialized. Here is the story.

Through the generosity of the late Dr. S. S. Royster, the
sum of $13,000 was given to the College for the establish-

ment of the Gardner-Webb College Community Health
Center, today commonly known as the Gardner-Webb
Clinic. With further donations from members of Dr.
Royster's family and from interested residents of Boiling
Springs and nearby communities, the Royster Memorial
Building was erected in 1949. The College built the build-
ing at a total cost of $21,500 from plans drawn by Van
Wageningen and Cothran, Shelby architects. The twelve-
bed building of brick construction was equipped with a
"large, light, and airy room for deliveries," a nursery, a
maternity room, a laboratory, a fully equipped kitchen,
an x-ray room, receiving and treatment rooms, nurses'
quarters, and three baths. The building of the Royster
Memorial Building was supervised by Belton G. Beason,
Cleveland County business man; and the architects and
several builders admitted that Mr. Beason's ingenius method of getting materials and work donated had resulted in
a building and equipment worth at least $35,000, had all
the work been done by contract. A number of donations
were made by individuals and churches in the area; and
rooms were furnished by the families of B. G. Beason, the
late W. W. Washburn, the Boiling Springs Lions Club, the
Boiling Springs Baptist Church, and the Green Bethel
Baptist Church, the local Negro church.

The Gardner-Webb College Community Health Center
opened for patients on December 1, 1949. The first patient
was Mrs. Evans McSwain of Route 3, Shelby; and the first
child born in the Health Center was her daughter Emily
Jean. The personnel was limited in the beginning: Dr.
Washburn was administrator; Mrs. Jane Jolley, College
nurse and head nurse; Mrs. Emily Washburn, graduate
nurse; Mrs. Ruth Hamrick, receptionist and bookkeeper;
and Miss Flossie Slater, a student with some training in
practical nursing. This small staff finished out 1949, but
early the next year others were added. The staff has continued to increase until in 1955-56 it numbered twenty—
two physicians, six full-time graduate nurses, three part-
time graduate nurses, four technicians and bookkeepers,

four nurses' aids, and one orderly.

The two physicians—Dr. Willard Wyan Washburn and Dr. Sam J. Crawley, Jr.,—are both natives of Cleveland County. Dr. Washburn, the son of Mr. and Mrs. J. C. Washburn of Route 4, Shelby, is a graduate of Wake Forest College and the Jefferson Medical College of Philadelphia. Following his internship at the North Carolina Baptist Hospital, he spent three years in the United States Army Medical Corps. In July of 1952, Dr. Sam J. Crawley, Jr., became associated with Dr. Washburn in the practice of medicine. The son of Mr. and Mrs. Sam J. Crawley of Lattimore, N. C., he attended Gardner-Webb College, Appalachian State Teachers College, and Wake Forest College. After serving four years in the United States armed forces during World War II, he began the study of medicine at the Bowman-Gray School of Medicine of Wake Forest College, from which he received an M.D. degree in 1951. Following a year's internship at Philadelphia General Hospital in Philadelphia, he came to Boiling Springs.

But there is still more to the story. In 1953, the Health Center was enlarged from twelve to twenty beds with other facilities for examination, diagnosis, and extra office space being added. This addition and the new equipment added cost approximately $25,000—$5000 of which was contributed by the Royster family. Approximately $8,000 was borrowed from the Hamrick Fund of the Memorial Building Fund, a sum on which Dr. Washburn paid the interest until the Hamrick Fund was repaid in full. Other funds came from residents of Boiling Springs and from other interested people.

Each year the Health Center and Dr. Washburn and Dr. Crawley use six to eight premedical and prenursing students in a program of self-help to enable the students to earn their way through college. They also offer preceptorships in their practice and in the Health Center for undergraduate medical students. An average year at the Health Center would find 1500 patients admitted, 225 babies delivered, 400 minor operations, including tonsillectomies, 18,000 out-patients seen by the two doctors, and 430 or more physical examinations given students at Gardner-Webb College. The operating budget is $45,000. In an average year, the Health Center will do $5,000 worth of charity work; and the doctors will give $10,000 worth of such free medical service.

From the beginning, the Health Center has sought to offer twenty-four hour medical care for all, complete diagnostic service second to none in its class, complete medical care for from 95-97% of all the people who visited the Health Center's two physicians, prenatal and postnatal care for mother and baby, delivery of babies and their care, general hospital medical care and minor surgery, cancer seminars, and assistance in the Red Cross blood program and polio vaccinations. In addition, the Health Center has, since its opening, offered a complete student health program for the students of Gardner-Webb College. This includes a complete examination and all indicated follow-up examinations, blood tests when there is an indicated need for one, vaccination for smallpox, typhoid, epidemic influenza, and tetanus, all professional care, calls, and consultations throughout the year, either in or out of the Health Center, required by the students, care for all athletic injuries, all ordinary medicines without charge to the student, hospitalization and minor surgery for all students at no cost to the student, and consultations and vocational guidance. And thus another of President Phil Elliott's dreams of Gardner-Webb College's serving the total area of which it is a part came to fruition.

On August 31, 1950, one of the best laid schemes of mice or men ever devised in Cleveland County, to echo Robert Burns, did not go astray in spite of the rains that came. On that day the Shelby Lions Club staged a Miracle Farm Day at the Gardner-Webb College Farm, a project that Joe Craver, soil conservationist for the Broad River District, estimated would increase the value of the property by $60,000 to $80,000 in a single day's operation.

Plans were carried out by seventeen special committees under the over-all direction of General Chairman Dathia Elliott. A lengthy list of distinguished men were invited by the Shelby Lions Club to be present to watch 182 acres be transformed into a modern farm in a single day. They were United States Secretary of Agriculture Charles F. Brannan, Governor W. Kerr Scott of North Carolina, North Carolina State Commissioner of Agriculture L. Y. "Stag" Ballentine, United States Senator Clyde R. Hoey, United States Senator Frank Porter Graham, Congressman A. L. Bulwinkle, Senator-nominate Willis Smith, and Congressman-nominate Woodrow Jones.

Plans were to clear, fertilize, and plant approximately 100 acres for cattle and hog pastures. Of these 100 pasture acres, 33 would have to be cleared by bulldozers of stumps from which timber had been harvested for lumber and pulpwood. About 75 acres of small grain were to be sown and a 2-acre fish pond dug. It was estimated, if all plans were to be carried out, that 35 bulldozers, 5 ten-yard dirt pans, 6 crawler-type tractors with heavy duty disc harrows, 35 farm tractors—15 of which should be equipped with rippers, 10 with bush and bogg harrows, and 10 with smoothing harrows—, 30 farm tractors—8 of which should be equipped with drag harrows, 8 with lime spreaders, 2 with wheat drills, 10 with culti-packers, and 2 with posthole diggers—, and one smaller tractor with a grass seeder would be needed.

Help came from many and varied sources. Certain portions of the work had to be done in advance of the August 31 spectacle, and there were willing hands to do the job. For example, 350 carpenters, mechanics, masons, and cabinet makers from the Vocational Department of the Blacksburg, S. C., Centralized High School offered their services in preparing the barn and poultry house. Their proffer of their services was accepted. The Blacksburg ex-GI volunteers came in two groups—225 in the morning and 125 in the afternoon—bringing with them their own hammers, saws, squares, and rulers. Watching the seem-

ingly endless line of men hammering and sawing in and
out of the barn's framing, H. L. Swain, director of the
group, said, "This is the biggest thing the boys have ever
worked on, the biggest project of this type. I understand
they don't want us to put anything up, though we could
with such a crew as this; but we're to leave the heavy
finishing work for the Miracle Day."

Materials as well as services were given. Twelve lumber
firms in Gaston, Lincoln, Rutherford, and Cleveland
Counties and two Shelby hardware companies agreed to
give needed supplies. For instance, the Z. J. Thompson
Lumber Company of Shelby agreed to furnish all doors
and windows needed in the project. The Shelby Supply
Company agreed to furnish all the Glidden paint and
brushes necessary for the entire project, and the Cleveland
Hardware Company of Shelby promised to give the needed
finished hardware and all the wallpaper for decorating the
renovated farm house. In addition, Lyman Martin and
Billy Beason, two well-known Cleveland County cabinet
makers, planned to install the finished kitchen storage units
as part of the renovation of the old farm house.

The old farm house, then nearly a century old, presented a combination of interesting, quaint, and perplexing
problems for project supervisor Joe Z. Blanton and his
assistants. The $4000 renovation was initiated by replacing
two heating and cooking chimneys with modern cooking
and dinette facilities. The workmen found that square
homemade nails had been used in the construction of the
house and that the old doors were paneled by hand and
were secured by wooden pegs. According to Mr. Blanton,
such pegs were seldom used after 1870, and Mr. Blanton
was sure that all the wood for the house was sawed on an
up-and-down saw, a type of saw popular long before the
turn of the century. But all agreed that it was a fine house
in its day. The hall and room walls were originally plas-
tered with mud and sand with perhaps the addition of a
little lime and white sand for the finishing coat. "In a way,
they went at everything backwards," Mr. Blanton ob-

served. "Look at that ceiling and the wall plaster smacked up against it. They put up the ceiling before the wall plaster, and the base boards before the plaster, making it mighty hard to put a polished finish on any sand and paper job we might try to do. But it has served a long time." Like many houses of its day, the original structure was a two-story frame building with four rooms and two halls, downstairs and up, with a rear wing being added later to form a typical L-shaped house. Renovation plans called for the kitchen and dinette, stripped by the workmen of the original fireplaces and partitions, to be refloored with inlaid linoleum and to be finished in knotty pine and tile board. Standard kitchen equipment was to be put in, including an electric stove and refrigerator given by Sears, Roebuck of Shelby. Wiring for the new equipment and for the entire house was to be donated by the Canipe Electric Company of Shelby.

The Shelby Lions Club found in Grady Cole, radio station WBT's colorful farm commentator, a willing and enthusiastic master of ceremony for the Miracle Farm Day. He came early to look over the farm. "You know," he said, "old Cleveland and Rutherford, these rolling hills and those blue mountains yonder, make two mighty pretty counties." He continued: "You know, lots of people are going to come a long ways to see this thing. Why, there'll be some people who will be here at the first dirt pushing, and they'll stay right down to the sunset. Tell 'em all you want to, write all you want to, but they like to see for themselves. That's the evidence for them, and that's what makes great things like this, and our people great." Leaning against the back of a truck, he drawled on, "A lot of people will come just to see the big Caterpillars push all those trees down that hill and over that crest, and others will watch the chicken house being finished up and equipped. . . . Some will follow our mobile jeep to hear the different jobs explained as they progress. But folks will watch what they want to watch, not what anybody tells them to watch. That's the American in them."

The rains came between 8 and 9 o'clock on August 31, but so did the people. Secretary of Agriculture Charles F. Brannan went right on with his scheduled address, which was described as a "rousing speech on the relationship of agriculture to democracy." So did North Carolina Governor W. Kerr Scott, who spoke briefly from the farmhouse porch in the early afternoon. During his noon lunch in the Gardner Memorial Student Union, Secretary Brannan said, "Gardner-Webb impresses me as a very fine institution," and Governor Scott declared, "I've ridden by here before, but have never before been on the campus. The physical development of Gardner-Webb has been great, but the spirit of the campus impresses me even more." Senator-nominate Willis Smith explained that his particular interest in the institution was due partly to his friendship with Ambassador Gardner and also to the fact that he had many Cleveland County friends. "The signs of substantial development being made by Gardner-Webb pleases me greatly. What I've seen in this short length of time impresses me," he said. The prominent Washington, D. C., attorney and law partner of Ambassador Gardner, Dr. Fred Morrison, accompanied Secretary Brannan. He referred to his being on the survey committee back when O. Max Gardner first took an interest in revitalizing the school. "We looked earnestly for what the community needed in college facilities," he explained. "And three years ago I helped with another survey committee through President Elliott, and now I return to find such buildings as the Gardner Memorial and Decker Hall for men completed. The results are highly impressive, and the future looks bright for such a college carefully planned for a specific service."

But all was not talk and encomium; a lot of hard work was done. Before the sun dropped behind the Blue Ridge Mountains in the distance, much of the following had been completed: 100 acres of land cleared, sown in permanent pasture, and fenced; 75 acres of land prepared and sown in small grain; one cattle barn, 52 feet by 96 feet, completed; a cement-block chicken house, 100 feet by 40 feet, erected; four farrowing houses erected; one 24-foot well dug and the pump installed; one six-room tenant house completely renovated, including wiring and plumbing; and a fish pond built.

It is interesting to note that, at one time, the land comprising the Gardner-Webb Miracle Farm was "a center of civilization in the southwestern part of Cleveland County," or so it has been described. The renovated farm house was built and owned by Captain Oliver Holland. There he, his wife, the former Miss Roxanna Hamrick, and their three children, Permelia, Williamson, and A. B., lived. Just to the rear of the Holland house stood the Holland School. The community consisted of Nicholson's post-office, Sid Settlemire's store, a mill, a cotton gin, and a buggy shop. Captain Holland was a unique character in his day, and many of his "sayings" were remembered long after he was gone. For thirty years—after returning from the War Between the States, in which he served as a Confederate officer—he was county magistrate and tax collector. On one occasion he ran for the State Legislature and lost by only ten votes. On the same porch from which the dignitaries spoke on Miracle Farm Day, the magistrate of years gone by tried many cases and married many couples. In its heyday, the old Holland place was filled with life and interest. In May came the "school-breaking." To the old Holland place came friends and relatives for candy pullings and old-fashioned parlor dancing. The fox was chased over the hills and hollows and along the banks of the Broad River, and Captain Holland had a special horse he used on the hunts. After Captain Holland's death in 1912, the land was sold to the Haynes family of Cliffside, N. C., then to the Cliffside Mills, and in 1945 to Gardner-Webb College.

There was one person whom the Miracle Farm did not cause to look backward. To President Phil Elliott it was a sign of the future, a harbinger of another significant step in the direction of a more fully realized community concept of education. To him, modern machinery signified only the manifestation of an intelligent grasp of human problems and the power and inventive genius to meet them. A number of by-products, President Elliott felt, would come to the College either directly or indirectly from the Miracle Farm Day. In the first place, it would bring a wider and deeper interest in the College itself, and people would come to realize more fully that the College belonged to no one in particular. In fact, it belonged to the Methodists as well as to the Baptists; to the Lutherans and Presbyterians, as well as to other religious groups in the area. It belonged, President Elliott insisted, to the bankers and farmers, to the employers and employees, and to the children born and unborn. It belonged to all who could see and appreciate its value. To President Elliott, the Miracle Farm Day also signaled the launching of what he called "certainly one of the most significant projects ever undertaken in this area of the country." He had reference to the establishment at Gardner-Webb College of a Department of Church-Community Development to be directed by "one of the ablest leaders in rural community development in the South."

The able leader was the Reverend Garland A. Hendricks, at that time pastor of the Olive Chapel Baptist Church, six miles west of Apex, N. C. Bringing with him an abundance of records and personal experiences in the field of community-church relations, he was to begin his new work on November 1, 1950. A short time before, Mr. Hendricks had published his BIOGRAPHY OF A COUNTRY CHURCH, the story of the Olive Chapel Church. A church, he felt, could not be separated from the community, nor the community from the church, if either was to live long or healthily. And as he put it, "Country people have the natural resources, and they can do when they see what they can do. There are thousands of churches in the South, in the two Carolinas, waiting for ideas and patterns to work by. As far as possible, that's what we hope to do at Gardner-Webb—give some ideas and patterns. We don't intend to tell anyone what to do. We are merely offering our discoveries in church-community growth to anyone who would like to apply them. Leading Southern ministers and laymen have told me such a college program has a bright future." And the future was bright, both for Mr. Hendricks and the Church-Community Development program. Repeatedly he was recognized as the outstanding man in the field of rural church sociology in the Southern Baptist Convention. In 1951, for example, he delivered a series of lectures in his field at the Southwestern Baptist Theological Seminary, Fort Worth, Texas; at the Northern Baptist Rural Church Conference, Green Lake, Wisconsin; at Carson-Newman College, Jefferson City, Tennessee; and at Texas A. and M. College, College Station, Texas.

For five years or more, President Elliott had been thinking of a program somewhat like the one Mr. Hendricks was to inaugurate. In December of 1945, President Elliott received the following letter from Assistant Executive Secretary Courts Redford of the Home Mission Board of the Southern Baptist Convention:

Dear President Elliott:

I am glad to have your letter of December 7 inviting me to visit Gardner-Webb College and explain to you and others interested in the promotion of our country church program the plan that is being followed by the Home Mission Board.

And now, five years later, the program was to start. But with all of his experience in rural church sociology, Garland Hendricks did not plunge directly into the task of setting up the program. Rather he and Executive Assistant to the President Ben Fisher visited eight Southern states in November of 1950. They studied the program of the Sunday School Board of the Southern Baptist Convention and discussed the possibilities of the projected Gardner-Webb program with A. V. Washburn, Jr., J. N. Barnette, and W. A. Harrill—each of whom pledged his full cooperation in the project. They conferred with the

President and several members of the faculty of Southern Baptist College, Walnut Ridge, Arkansas, where an experiment had been tried in adult education on the campus. The Gardner-Webb plans and possibilities were discussed with several Protestant denominational leaders at meetings of the National Rural Church Convocation at Columbia, Missouri. A study of the Howard College extension program was made; and Dr. S. F. Dowis of the Home Mission Board, Atlanta, Georgia, assured the support of the Home Mission Board in the projected Church-Community Development program.

Back at Gardner-Webb, a meeting devoted to a discussion of the development of the rural church was held on December 13. Cooperating with Gardner-Webb in this undertaking were the Rural Church Department of the North Carolina Baptist State Convention and Wake Forest College. Dr. Ralph A. Felton of Drew University, one of the outstanding rural church leaders in America, emphasized the seven essentials of a rural church program: resident teaching, in-service training, research, the conducting of extension classes, experimental parishes, legislation, and the production of literature. The Reverend Henry E. Walden, Jr., Secretary of the Rural Church Department of the North Carolina Baptist State Convention, called attention to the fact that, of the 2500 Baptist churches in North Carolina, 1800 were in the open country and 400 were in villages of less than 500 population. H. A. Hopkins discussed the rural church program of Howard College in Alabama, showing how "a Baptist college takes its program to the people." In the afternoon, Mr. Fisher presented the rural church program of Gardner-Webb College to the group, and Mr. Hendricks addressed the group on "How Our Small Communities Work for the Lord."

Early in 1951, Garland Hendricks began to map out a research and experiment project for the Department of Church-Community Development—a project reflecting the experience Garland Hendricks brought to the task and the meticulous care which he determined to devote to the task. A five-year plan of work, to extend from July 1, 1951 through June 30, 1956, was carefully outlined in detail. North Carolina, the area for study, was, so it was pointed out, a state of small communities where decentralized industry and diversified agriculture gave an opportunity for the creation of the best balanced economy in the United States. The purpose of the research was "to accumulate the best ideas available on the work of churches in agricultural and industrial communities, arranging the subject matter so as to picture a profile of North Carolina, a profile of the types of communities in North Carolina, and the role of the church in the agricultural and industrial communities." Once this picture was assembled, it was to be made available, in digest form, to persons in positions of leadership.

There existed a positive need for such a study. The amazing development of industry and large cities in the Western world, so the outline stated, blinded people to the significance of the small community. The significance of the small community should now be recognized; and the church and the community should be more closely related than ever before, for the church is the principal social agency in the small community. S. H. Hobbs, Jr., in CHURCH AND COMMUNITY IN THE SOUTH declares that "the rural church should emphasize a better social and economic life for the community through better farming, soil conservation, and improved recreational facilities." The church is also the strongest motivating force, the outline went on to say, in the small community. The rural people can give to their church the largest part of their time allotted to organizations; and, consequently, "the quality of rural society may be said to depend largely on the complexion of the rural church." There is also reason to believe that the physical, mental, and moral strength of a people is related to the quality of the soil that supports it. Thus the church may rightly concern itself with the very dust of the earth. In fact, "the divine purpose

demands an intelligent interpretation and dynamic application of religion in the human scene in order that man
may be assured of a true direction in life."

How would such a research and experiment project be
carried out? There were already some churches engaged
in a successful ministry to their communities. A special
study would be made of them. Books would be purchased;
leading newspapers and magazines would be subscribed to;
researchers were to be sent to selected libraries for special
study of periodicals, journals, out-of-print books, unpublished theses and dissertations, and other pertinent material.
An effort would be made to secure bulletins of churches
and publications of church councils, conferences, and associations. The fruits of the research were then to be edited
and copy prepared for distribution to interested church
and civic leaders, farm and industrial leaders, business and
financial leaders, as well as to members of Chambers of
Commerce, rural sociologists, and teachers of rural church
work. In the Dover Memorial Library of Gardner-Webb
College, the best available books in the field and a special
file of materials were to be collected and made available
for on-the-premises research.

To make a thorough study of this kind would take, it
was estimated, at least five years. This did not mean that
the Department of Church-Community Development
would devote all of its resources to making the study or
that its program would wait until the results of the study
were available. By no means. In fact, in January, 1951,
the Department, to provide a teaching ministry in regular
college classes for students on the campus, included two
courses in the curriculum of the College—A Church at
Work, a study of what a church is and how it may be
organized for the purpose of bearing an effective witness,
with special attention being given to designing and executing a program of work which will develop Christian character in people and minister to human needs in a community; and Community Building, a survey of the structure of community life in the South to enable the student

to see how citizens may work for community betterment through various organizations and institutions. In January also, night classes in adult Christian education began on the Gardner-Webb campus, where courses in the Bible, Church Music, Church Organizations, and A Church at Work were offered. Between January, 1951, and May, 1952, no less than 636 persons from 135 churches were enrolled in these on-campus night courses. In 1952 other night classes, off the campus but similar to the on-campus ones, were sponsored jointly by the College and five different Baptist Associations—Catawba River, South Fork, Gaston, Green River, and Ebenezer, a Negro Association— with an aggregate enrollment of 794 from 128 churches. By the time of its progress report in May of 1952, the Department had placed 230 new books in the College library for the use of students, pastors, and church leaders. Some time before—in November of 1951—the Department published the first issue of a four-paged quarterly bulletin, which described projects that would improve church and community life—a bulletin that was mailed each quarter to all Baptist pastors in North Carolina and South Carolina, to some 200 laymen interested in church-community development, and to Baptist leaders in twenty states. The purpose of the bulletin, entitled *Church-Community Development*, according to its first issue, was stated thusly: "By sharing ideas with one another in the traditional patterns of democratic choice and action, we can learn how to put these resources to work for the growth of character and development of communities."

Under the direction of Dr. Robert Allen Dyer, another valuable college and community asset was developed—the Department of Guidance. On the campus, it afforded each student an opportunity for a personal appraisal of his ability, personality, interests, and aptitude and, in addition, vocational guidance and counseling in keeping with his ability, interests, and talents. To accomplish its purposes, the Department developed a basic testing program of general ability inventories, personality inventories, and individually supervised aptitude tests to be followed by personal counseling and guidance given by trained personnel. In line with the College's purpose to extend its services to the community, a program of vocational testing and guidance was also made available to high school students in three counties and personal counseling was made available to the communities and agencies of the area—services of which the communities were glad to take advantage. For example, one year Dr. Dyer offered night courses in Psychology of Human Relations—two hours one night each week for fifteen weeks—to 30 supervisors and other officials of the Cleveland Cloth Mills; and for twelve weeks, he taught the same course to 25 supervisors and top management personnel of the Spindale Mills. At the Rutherford Hospital School of Nursing, Rutherfordton, N. C., Dr. Dyer, the examiner recognized by the National League for Nursing for the Gastonia, Shelby, Morganton, Rutherfordton area, administered ability, personality, and vocational inventories, graded them, and compiled the data for 53 student nurses. He then spent eleven days in personal counseling with this group. In addition, he administered the entrance testing program to three different groups of prospective students for this hospital during the year. Three entrance tests were given to three groups of prospective nurses at the Shelby Hospital; and two different groups of prospective student nurses were tested at Gastonia Hospital. Dr. Dyer also counseled with the hospital personnel at Gastonia relative to the selection of its student nurses. Dr. Dyer's services were likewise available to parents of problem children in Cleveland and Rutherford Counties, and he undertook the testing and counseling of retarded children for the Cleveland and Rutherford County public school systems. And at a special High School Day held on the campus for students from high schools of the surrounding area, the Department of Guidance tested 128 students and spent 112 hours in compiling the data which were sent to the high school guidance counselors.

In April of 1951, Dr. Jesse P. Bogue, Executive Secretary of the American Association of Junior Colleges and author of the book, THE COMMUNITY COLLEGE, visited Gardner-Webb College for a series of conferences and forums with the faculty and trustees. This was following a policy laid down some time before by the administration and Board of Trustees of inviting top men in the field of education for consultation about the College program. The conferences opened with a brief summary of the rise and growth of the junior college in American education. There followed discussion groups in curriculum problems, public relations, finance, vocational training, and adult education. Dr. Bogue was hearty in his approbation, to borrow a phrase from Dale Carnegie, of Gardner-Webb's Community Health Center, Church-Community Development program, and Department of Guidance. Of the Church-Community Development program, he said, "It is the best planned and most practical approach to this problem which I have yet seen," and only one other school in the nation and that at Boise, Idaho, he pointed out, had such a program as that offered by the Community Health Center.

Complacency has never characterized President Elliott's administration. Thinking, weighing alternatives, and moving forward when the time seemed right has. In his Annual Report to the Board of Trustees, May 23, 1951, President Elliott discussed three projects which were or had been under consideration but had "not been launched as yet." And to this day they have not been launched, but the fact that they were considered reveals something of the constant search that the administration and Trustees are making to expand the services and usefulness of the College. One of these was expansion to include vocational subjects. Perhaps the Miracle Farm rekindled the vocational emphasis. Late in the summer of 1950, President Elliott, in discussing the uses to which the Miracle Farm would be put, said that the College for some time had been "working on a plan of study for those who will end their formal training here. It is a three-year course, awarding for its completion the Associate in Rural Life diploma. This course will require certain basic information and skills in agriculture. The farm will facilitate that program." In his Annual Report to the Trustees, President Elliott referred to the expense of vocational education but indicated that he felt the College could expand in this direction to a great extent if a service program of cooperation with the businesses and textile industries of the area could be worked out "whereby people could work a season and go to school for a period." "In this way," President Elliott said, "we can raise the intellectual level of employees and thereby increase both the quality and quantity of their production and service."

It had also been suggested that Gardner-Webb undertake to become a three- or four-year junior college vertically integrated. But President Elliott warned that the proposal was "an innovation of a very revolutionary nature, and could well do great damage. It would do damage unless we see clearly what we are after, and are convinced of its relative worth." President Elliott was concerned with "lifting the quality of . . . work all along the lines" and of following the "expressed policy of the College" in making "changes on the basis of research."

Suggested too was expansion upward into a four-year senior college. Perhaps few felt the time right for such an undertaking in 1951, although no doubt some approved the idea as the College faculty was also to do some few years later.

Before the opening of the 1951 football season, Gardner-Webb, along with Asheville-Biltmore Junior College, Mars Hill Junior College, Lees-McRae Junior College, Spartanburg Junior College, and North Greenville Junior College, withdrew from the old Carolinas Junior College Conference and formed the new Western Carolina Junior College

Athletic Association. The Gardner-Webb Bulldogs accommodated themselves so well to their new environment that, for the first time in the history of the College, the football squad completed an undefeated season. Along with the splendid record came an invitation to play in the second Golden Isles Bowl at Brunswick, Georgia, on November 30 against South Georgia Junior College for the benefit of underprivileged children. The faculty approved the invitation. The team went, but this time it did not conquer. It lost 6-0. A year and another similar invitation later, however, the situation proved to be different, and the Bulldogs defeated Georgia Military College of Milledgeville, Georgia, 14-0 in the third annual Golden Isles Bowl before 4000 people at Brunswick's Lanier Field.

Spring, 1952, came; May came; the John R. Dover Memorial Library was nearing completion; and plans for its dedication on Sunday afternoon, May 25, had been made. Originally, the dedicatory ceremony was to have been held on the terrace of the O. Max Gardner Memorial Building; but because of a blazing summer sun, some plans were changed, and Grover H. Jones, then President of the North Carolina Baptist State Convention and a prominent High Point, N. C., lawyer, delivered the principal address in the E. B. Hamrick Auditorium. Preceding the address, the Reverend John S. Farrar, pastor of the Boiling Springs Baptist Church, delivered the invocation; and the College a capella choir, directed by Professor Stephen Morrisett, sang. The Reverend Ben C. Fisher, Executive Assistant to the President, made an address of welcome; and Claude F. Gaddy, Executive Secretary of the Council on Christian Education of the North Carolina Baptist State Convention, brought greetings from the Baptist colleges and institutions of North Carolina. Formal presentation of the $160,000 building was made, on behalf of the Dover family, by Charles I. Dover, Secretary and Treasurer of the Dover Mills—a building erected as a memorial to his father, the late John R. Dover, Cleveland County industrialist, churchman, civic leader, and life-long supporter of Christian education. The building was accepted on behalf of the Gardner-Webb Board of Trustees by Mrs. Rush Stroup, on behalf of the College administration by President Phil Elliott, and on behalf of the students by Glenn Henson, President of the Student Body.

Several special collections to be housed in the new library were presented to the College and were accepted by Miss Carolyn Wray, librarian. Lee B. Weathers, publisher of the Shelby *Star*, formally presented the Thomas Dixon Collection—a collection now housed partially in the Cleveland Shrine Room and a collection that the College had received several years before. Clarence Griffin, publisher of the Forest City *Courier*, gave the College the North Carolina Collection of History and Publications, which is now housed in the North Carolina Room of the library. Jay Jenkins, then on the staff of the Raleigh *News and Observer* but now director of the Raleigh Bureau of the Charlotte *Observer*, presented his gift of the John Charles McNeill Collection to the College; and the Reverend Garland Hendricks presented the North Carolina Grange Collection on Rural Life.

Following the prayer of dedication by the Reverend John W. Suttle, oldest active member of the Board of Trustees, the Marshals of the College led the Dover family, the College administration and faculty, the Trustees, and special guests to the entrance of the spacious and beautifully furnished library, at which time the doors were formally opened, and the group toured the building.

With the addition of the Dover Memorial Library—the "heart" of the campus—someone whose heart could never be far away from the campus retired in the summer of 1952. That someone was Mrs. J. D. Huggins, Sr., who retired, as someone put it, "knowing her beloved school will continue under capable and consecrated leadership to train boys and girls from farms, towns, and cities in the spirit of Christianity." The daughter of James Bennet

Atkins and Mary Susan Hogue Atkins of York County, S. C., she attended Pine Grove High School and Erskine College, where she received her A.B. degree. Her first teaching was in Bethany High School in her native York County. There she met, fell in love with, and married J. D. Huggins, who also was, at the time, teaching in the school. The young couple came in 1907 to Boiling Springs, to a community and to a school that received the full measure of their devotion, with the exception of one year they spent at Mooresboro, until Professor Huggins' death in 1932 and singly of her devotion and love and interest since.

On September 24, 1952, President Phil Elliott announced that a campaign directed by Ben Fisher for $60,000 would be launched immediately. The campaign, to be pushed during the academic year 1952-53, was designed to be a combined project for Living Endowment, for current operations, for operational expenses of the Church-Community Development program, for work scholarships for students, and for debt retirement. One of the pressing needs just then was for $15,000 for work scholarships and student aid since, it was declared, approximately one-fourth of the students—both men and women—attending Gardner-Webb could not remain in college unless some means of self-help were provided.

Perhaps inspired by the campaign for $60,000 but more than likely motivated by an interest in the education of gifted but financially handicapped young people, Holt MacPherson and Mrs. MacPherson in November of 1952 set up a special scholarship fund to encourage superior freshmen from the Shelby area to enter Gardner-Webb. Like his close personal friend, the late Ambassador Gardner, Holt MacPherson seemed especially eager that Gardner-Webb attract the finest caliber of student possible. According to Charles I. Dover, then Chairman of the College Board of Trustees, the initial gift of stock in radio station WOHS in Shelby had a value in excess of $10,000, and the donor had expressed his purpose to add to the fund with further gifts if its usefulness developed. There was also a secondary purpose of the fund, and that was to encourage exceptional students to transfer, after their period of study at Gardner-Webb, to accredited colleges and universities. The MacPhersons' gift climaxed more than a decade of service to the College, and it provoked warm praise from the College administration. President Elliott, expressing his gratitude for the gift, said, "The recent decision of Holt MacPherson to return to the editorship of the High Point *Enterprise* is a great loss to Gardner-Webb, but we are gratified to see this manifestation of his abiding interest in the school and the development of its students. Throughout my entire administration he has been one of our staunchest supporters, and he had been untiring in his efforts in behalf of our college."

On December 1, 1952, the news that the Executive Assistant to the President of Gardner-Webb College, Ben Fisher, had resigned was made public. A month later, Mr. Fisher was to assume his dual duties as Executive Secretary of the Department of Christian Education of the General Association of Baptists in Kentucky and as Associate to the Executive Secretary of the Education Commission of the Southern Baptist Convention. The shadow Ben Fisher cast was an especially big one. He could not but be missed, and that on a large scale, for, directly or indirectly, he had directed campaigns and solicited funds that brought in thousands of dollars for Gardner-Webb College. During Mr. Fisher's service as Director of the Gardner-Webb College Department of Public Relations, the $250,000 Endowment Fund Campaign was completed, the $35,000 drive for the President's home was completed, the campaign to raise the remainder of the $238,000 necessary to pay for the James Webb Gardner Dormitory was successfully concluded, the Living Endowment program was instituted, and 300,000 pieces of literature on every phase of college work were published. In addition, Mr. Fisher handled the promotion, through the Department of Public Relations, of the College Health Center which led to the procuring of a building and equipment valued in excess of $50,000. He also handled the promotion of the Miracle Farm Day, "whose benefit [sic] to Gardner-Webb College has been estimated at $75,000 to $100,000." Mr. Fisher's value to Gardner-Webb, however, can not be assayed altogether in dollars and cents. For instance, under his direction the Alumni work was reorganized and quarterly publications initiated; the News Bureau was established; and Mr. Fisher worked along with others in developing the Church-Community Development program and the College's adult education program. He developed a systematic student procurement program, produced a complete set of Kodachrome slides to be used in the promotion of the College and aided in the filming of a 16-mm sound-color film entitled "A College at Work," depicting the curricula, facilities, faculty, and students of Gardner-Webb College "at work"—a film produced by the Council on Christian Education of the North Carolina Baptist State Convention to promote the work of Christian Education in North Carolina.

So much were the Trustees impressed with the services of Ben Fisher to the College that, to express their appreciation, they presented him with an engraved tribute on sheep-skin, which read, "We especially pay tribute to him for his enlistment of financial contributions, moral support, and special help exceeding the community support of any denominational school of its size in the South." The tribute was signed by Charles I. Dover, Lee B. Weathers, and Ralph Webb Gardner.

Garland Hendricks too was shortly to resign from the Gardner-Webb faculty and to accept an appointment to the faculty of the Southeastern Baptist Seminary at Wake Forest, N. C. His resignation was publicly announced on February 23. This meant, of course, that he would not get to finish the five-year plan he had mapped out for the Church-Community Development program. However, President Elliott, in discussing Mr. Hendricks' going to his new duties as Associate Professor of Church-Community Development at the Seminary, indicated that the work started by Mr. Hendricks was to be continued and that he hoped soon to anounce the appointment of a successor to Mr. Hendricks. To the Seminary Board of Trustees, President Elliot made this statement: "Although the faculty and trustees at Gardner-Webb feel that they have sustained a great loss, we feel humbly grateful that when a great graduate school like Southeastern needs the best man in the South for a great job, it would come to Gardner-Webb to find him. In my judgment, Mr. Hendricks has made at Gardner-Webb one of the outstanding Church-Community Development achievements in the South. I feel a great personal loss in his going." And about his own going, Mr. Hendricks had this to say: "It has been a thrilling experience to work with those who make Gardner-Webb College one of the finest schools anywhere. Everywhere there has been a cordial spirit, a genuine concern and evidence of prayerful interest which has made the work here delightful. Let me assure you that in our efforts at Southeastern Seminary we will work with Gardner-Webb and the churches of this area in every way possible."

Early in April, President Elliott announced simultaneously two appointments to fill the vacancies created by the resignations of Ben Fisher and Garland Hendricks. Both appointments were to be effective in May, 1953. The Reverend John Worth Long had been named to succeed Ben Fisher. Mr. Long, a native of Gastonia, N. C., had been educated at Gardner-Webb College, Wake Forest College, and the Crozer Theological Seminary, having been graduated with high honors from each institution. A veteran of World War II, he was born in Bowling Green, South Carolina, in the very month World War I ended. Mr. Long had held pastorates in North Carolina, Virginia, Maryland, and New Jersey. The other appointee, William Lawson Allen, was to return to Gardner-Webb as Mr. Hendricks' successor. A layman and son of a minister, Mr.

Allen was born at Bushnell, Swain County, North Carolina, in September, 1906. He received his education at Sylva Collegiate Institute, a Baptist mountain school, at Western Carolina Teachers College, at the University of Tennessee, at Southern Baptist Theological Seminary, and at Southwestern Baptist Theological Seminary. Mr. Allen brought with him to his new position a varied experience. For six years he worked for the United States Post Office Department, and for the Southern Railroad for two years. He taught in the high schools at Lewiston and Canton for another two years, and he spent two more years as a teacher in the Department of Religion and as Religious Director and Field Secretary at Gardner-Webb. For twelve years, he served as educational director in a number of outstanding churches, among them the First Baptist Churches of Jacksonville, Florida, Spartanburg, South Carolina, Asheville, North Carolina, and Winston-Salem, North Carolina.

President Phil Elliott was one, where his faculty was concerned, who followed Dale Carnegie's advice. He was "lavish in his praise and hearty in his approbation." Thus in the spring of 1953, he again told the Trustees that, to use his words, "the faculty at Gardner-Webb is outstanding." That is not to say that the faculty was a perfect paragon of what a faculty ought to be, and no one knew this better than the faculty members themselves. In fact, during the academic year 1952-53, the faculty, with President Elliott's approval, sought to evaluate the College personnel, the curriculum, the campus life, the athletic program, the physical equipment, and other aspects of the College program. Oh, to be sure, the faculty found many fine things to say about themselves—such as "a great faculty, highly trained, capable, and hungry for service." They did not, however, close their eyes to their shortcomings; but for this chronicler to enumerate their candidly expressed criticisms of themselves and others and to preserve such in printer's ink for posterity would be like washing one's dirty linen in public.

But President Elliott trusted his faculty, and this trust could not be more clearly demonstrated than in his turning the faculty loose to work out, in the spring of 1953, a faculty salary scale. Of course, President Elliott was close by to offer his counsel and advice; but the scale, as worked out, was a faculty job. "You work out a scale," the President told his faculty, "and I'll take it to the Trustees for you." The faculty members recommended, as one would have expected them to do, a salary scale, based upon academic training and experience, which quite likely would make them the highest paid faculty members in any junior college in North Carolina—that is, if it passed the Trustees as it was presented. This is not to say that it was unreasonable. Far from it. And when President Elliott laid the faculty-drafted salary scale before the Trustees, they did not whittle a mill from the proposed salaries for the various academic ranks. A few suggestions, however, relative to salaries to be paid in the summer session and Sabbatical leaves were perhaps just silently overlooked.

The President's Report to the Board of Trustees in May of 1953 was President Elliott's tenth one, and he reviewed the College's progress during this first decade of his administration. Ten years before, when first he walked onto the Gardner-Webb campus, the late Ambassador Gardner is reputed to have said to him, "You are the only man in North Carolina foolish enough to undertake this job." The fledgling President understood the hidden challenge of that statement when he glanced over the 35-acre campus and saw only five superannuated buildings. The financial condition of the College, the bedrock of any successful college operation, was anything but encouraging. The total assets of the College were valued at $297,866.26, of which $278,-099.64 was in land, buildings, and other things. The operating fund was a mere $5,871.53, and the scholarship fund totaled only $6,140.83, including the $5,000 recently placed in the fund by Governor Gardner. The endowment fund, a sort of hidden treasure in the form of stocks and bonds and other securities, amounted to $7,754.25. In 1952 (the 1952-53 audit was not yet available at the time of the President's Report) the total assets of the College were valued at $1,718,288.57, of which $1,381,122.99 was in land, buildings, and equipment. The operating fund was $68,609.07, and the scholarship fund now totaled $8,421.62. The College now had an endowment of $260,-134.89. In 1953, the College was accredited by the Southern Association of Colleges and Secondary Schools, the North Carolina College Conference, and the National Council on Education. The College was approved by the American Medical Association for two years of pre-medical training and by the United States government for the training of foreign students. The College also was a member of the American Association of Junior Colleges, the Southern Association of Junior Colleges, and the Southern Association of Baptist Colleges and Schools. The enrollment had increased from a total of 103 in 1943-44 to 424 in 1951-52.

But President Elliott stubbornly refused to accept credit for the phenomenal decade of growth. "I attribute the success of our progress," he said, "to three forces: the cooperation and assistance of our local businessmen and citizens, the loyalty of our trustees, and the unity and support of our faculty have made possible the growth of our college." And a decade of growth it was! Nineteen buildings were erected on the campus: two six-apartment buildings for married students, five duplex apartments, the President's home, the Health Center, four dormitory units (McMurry, Suttle, and Hoey-Anthony-Padgett-Young, and the James Webb Gardner Dormitory), the O. Max Gardner Memorial Student Union, the Dover Memorial Library, the $160,000 heating plant, the book store, and two steel quonset huts. But of it all, President Elliott said, "The physical growth is the least spectacular—it's the inner relations, the binding together of our entire community into a consolidated force for good that seems most gratifying."

Even yet the College needed more facilities; plans called for at least five more buildings—a science building, two more dormitories, an administration building, and a combination gymnasium-community recreation center. And academically also the College was not yet ready to rest on its laurels. It had no classes in organic chemistry, art, German, mechanical drawing, American literature, or agriculture; and the Music Department did not meet the standards of the American Schools of Music.

And another problem—shades of 1928!—loomed ominously near. President Elliott warned the Trustees that, in the foreseeable future, North Carolina would add the 13th and 14th grades to the secondary school system. He asserted that

When that time comes, the private junior colleges will face the alternatives of becoming so unique and outstanding in their programs and so entrenched financially that they can compete with the tax-supported schools; or they will close their doors. It is now time to face these problems realistically and dispassionately. When you add to the above the fact that not only the large private colleges, but also the tax-supported ones are, with their high-powered public relations department, combing every area of our potential support for additional aid for themselves, including millions to induce the best intellects to their campuses, the outlook is even less optimistic. It will take the best wisdom and dedication of all to meet our challenge and responsibility of preserving for tomorrow the indispensable small liberal arts college devoted to high scholarship and service.

Accepting the challenge and responsibility of making at least one small Christian liberal arts college as well equipped and efficient for tomorrow as it could, the Gardner-Webb College Board of Trustees, on November 1, 1953, endorsed the idea of a Golden Anniversary to be celebrated by the College in 1957. The project was handed on to the Executive Committee of the Trustees to work out. On February 8, 1954, the Trustees formally approved the observance of the Golden Anniversary and tied in with it an eight-point program designed to complete the building of the campus and to endow the College adequately by the time of the anniversary, three years in the future. First, the school's endowment was to be increased from approximately $260,000 to $1,000,000. The student loan fund also was to be increased from $10,600 to $40,000. Plans too called for the razing of the old Huggins-Curtis Building and the replacing of it with a modern combination administration-science building. Efforts would likewise be made to reach and maintain a student enrollment of 500. This would necessitate more dormitory accommodations—another dormitory for 50 boys and another dormitory for 100 girls. The plans, as announced, provided for the construction of a physical education building containing a swimming pool and for the completion of the athletic field. A definite need was felt for additional faculty housing, especially for single faculty members; and an eight-apartment building was projected. To beautify the campus, a beautification project to cost $20,000 and to include an outdoor theater rounded out the so-called eight-point program, which would necessitate for its realization a campaign to raise $1,750,000.

The Golden Anniversary plans were indeed ambitious ones. To head the campaign, Dr. H. Hansel Stembridge, Jr., pastor of the First Baptist Church of Forest City, N. C., was granted a partial leave of absence by his church. At a meeting of the Steering Committee of the Golden Anniversary Campaign, community leaders, and friends of the College at the Cleveland Country Club on Armistice Day, 1954, President Elliott reminded the group of the tremendous service Gardner-Webb was rendering to the people of North Carolina, adding that "the only limitation to what it can do is the limitation of tools and funds with which to work." The plans also took cognizance of the great influx of students which would be seeking college admission a few years hence—an avalanche of students which perhaps by 1960 would double the college enrollment of 1954. With greatly expanded facilities and living quarters, Gardner-Webb would be prepared to care for some of this demand in its area.

President Phil Elliott was busily about his multitudinous speaking engagements in the fall of 1954 when suddenly a heart condition arrested his activities. His doctor ordered him to bed for an enforced rest and recuperation. Some weeks later—on December 11—the Trustees granted President Elliott a three-months' leave of absence, and he prepared to spend the rest of the winter in Florida. W. Lawson Allen was appointed Acting President until President Elliott could once again assume his duties.

Gifts came and goals were accepted in the drive to raise the $1,750,000. In January, 1955, the largest single contribution from any one source—a gift of $36,000—was pledged by the congregation of the Boiling Springs Baptist Church to be paid in installments over a three-year period. The church planned to give $1000 each month for the following nine months, to give $12,000 a year for two full-year periods, and to make up the remaining $3000 along the way. On January 20, Dr. Stembridge announced that the College had received a challenge gift of $25,000 for the Golden Anniversary Expansion Fund from Mrs. O. Max Gardner, Sr., Ralph Webb Gardner, and O. Max Gardner, Jr., through the O. Max Gardner Foundation. It would be given as soon as an equal amount was on hand from other sources. By the middle of March, goals amounting to $593,000 had been accepted over a three-year period.

After more than 65 years as an active Baptist minister and after 43 consecutive years as an active member of the Board of Trustees of Boiling Springs High School, Boiling Springs College, and Gardner-Webb College, the Reverend John W. Suttle—the "Little Preacher," as he is affectionately called—retired. In January, 1955, the College Trustees approved plans to launch in April the $100,000 Suttle Memorial Endowment drive to endow the Church-Community Development program of the College. From 1890 to 1954, the "Little Preacher" had been pastor of 37 Baptist churches in North and South Carolina. For 28 years, he had been pastor of from five to seven churches at a time. He was pastor of five churches on his 80th birthday. In 1948, he was elected President of the North Carolina Baptist State Convention, but gave up the position after one year because of illness. For 40 years, he was Moderator of the Kings Mountain Baptist Association, a post from which he retired in 1952.

John William Suttle was born on April 7, 1872, in Cleveland County, one of seven children of Charles Beattie Suttle and Jane Wray Suttle. He grew up on a farm and vows that the reason he walks with a pronounced limp came from "cradling" so much wheat as a youth. He can recall vividly helping to raise the money that built the Memorial Building back in the rather financially lean days just after World War I. As he put it, "I volunteered to help with the construction of the new building, but they took one look at my 115 pounds and said I wouldn't be worth much as a hod carrier, and I didn't know how to do anything else. I heard they were running short on money, so I decided to help raise the necessary funds to pay for the building. I started out early one July morning to talk to prospective donors about the little Baptist school; it was a high school then, you know. I drove my horse and buggy all over the county, and I must have talked to 50 farmers and storekeepers that day. When I got home that night, I had $3.20 in cash, and 68 cents pledged. The only other good thing I got that day was a good dinner of fresh beans and corn bread and blackberry pie, and some fresh oats hay for my horse."

In the late summer of 1955, Dr. H. H. Stembridge announced that five counties had adopted Golden Anniversary goals totaling $810,000 for the three-year period. For instance, Cleveland County agreed to attempt to raise $300,000 by 1957. In September, Gaston County was to begin its drive toward a goal of $100,000. On October 23, under the leadership of Claude Hinson and the Reverend Walter Long, Belmont, Mount Holly, Cramerton,

and McAdenville were to launch their combined campaign
for $50,000. Kings Mountain and Bessemer City, under
the leadership of Arnold Kincaid, too were to combine
their efforts to raise $50,000.

The Golden Anniversary Campaign bore its first visible
fruit on Sunday, October 9, 1955. In an afternoon ceremony, presided over by President Phil Elliott, three former
Presidents of the College—Dr. Zeno Wall, the Reverend
J. R. Cantrell, and Horace Easom—turned the traditional
shovels of dirt at the groundbreaking for a new $250,000
girls' dormitory. The principal address was then delivered
by United States Senator Sam J. Ervin, Jr. Senator Ervin
said that the church-related college is essential to the well-
being of the church and of incalculable value to society.
"North Carolina cannot educate her youth without the
assistance of the church college," Senator Ervin said. "It
performs a role that cannot be done by state universities
in that it combines studies of Christianity with those of
the arts and sciences. State schools are limited in the study
of religion, but the church college keeps religion abreast
of life and life abreast of religion. The church receives
most of its pastors and leaders from the church college.
It is essential that these schools be maintained to strengthen
the role of the church." Senator Ervin maintained that
it was impossible to magnify to greatly the place of the
church-related college in North Carolina and that he
looked forward with confidence to Gardner-Webb's sending forth young men and women of the caliber of the
members of the two Cleveland County families whose
names the College bears.

Late in 1955 the Ford Foundation announced that it
would distribute millions of dollars to senior colleges and
non-profit agencies of colleges throughout the United
States. Gardner-Webb, like other junior colleges, did not
share in the gifts, but the Gardner-Webb Health Center
did. It received $10,900. Dr. Wyan Washburn and his
associate, Dr. Sam Crawley, Jr., indicated that the gift
was made in recognition of the pioneer work done by the

clinic as a community health center. About the gift, Dr. Washburn said, "I will recommend to the Committee [a special Hospital Committee] that the money be used in the extension of the service of the clinic to the community, possibly some of it in health education."

In his 1955 Report to the Board of Trustees, President Elliott declared that "the finance system of the College is sound." However, the normal income—that is, income from students, the North Carolina Baptist State Convention, and endowment—would not balance the budget. This was due, President Elliott pointed out, to three facts: 1. the inability to accommodate the maximum student body the faculty could teach; 2. the unique and outstanding service program to the community, the churches of the area, and the Baptist denomination; and 3. the outstanding, highly trained, and devoted faculty. The budget *could* be balanced, to be sure.. It could be balanced by *decreasing* quality and service along the line—or by taking more students. "Our greatest difficulty," President Elliott said, "is apathy. We must advance to maintain our balance. And we must never forget that all our equipment and means constitute but the tools with which teachers who love truth, their subjects, and boys and girls mould out of the students the Christian citizens of tomorrow."

As has been indicated elsewhere, President Elliott regards the crowning achievement of his administration to be the assembling at Gardner-Webb of a faculty that understands the needs of youth and that is devoted to the serious business of teaching without which all else would be meaningless. On March 8, 1956, President Elliott announced the merit promotion of two of his faculty. Hubert C. Dixon, who had taught mathematics in the College, with the exception of the War years, since 1935 and who had served at various times as Dean, Registrar, and Vice-President, was promoted from assistant professor to associate professor; and Paul J. Stacy, who joined the College faculty in 1941, was promoted to the rank of assistant professor.

"I know of no more loyal or deserving teachers," Dr. Elliott stated in announcing these promotions. "They represent the best in our faculty. Their service in the classroom has been outstanding, and their students consistently make good when they transfer to senior colleges." In addition to these two, both of whom had served the College more than 10 years, there were on the 1955-56 faculty seven who had taught in the College for a decade or more. Dr. Robert Allen Dyer, Director of Guidance, joined the faculty in 1946. James Young Hamrick, Dean of Men and Assistant Professor of English, came in 1945 as did James Stephen Morrisett, Head of the Department of Bible, and James O. Terrell, Dean of Instruction. Miss Abbie Miller, Chairman of the Department of Fine Arts, joined the faculty as a teacher of music in the fall of 1947—just one year after Mrs. Elma Estelle Harper Pollock, Chairman of the Modern Language Department, began her tenure on the College faculty. Dr. Thomas C. Holland taught in Boiling Springs High School from 1915-1917 and rejoined the faculty as a teacher in the College in 1945. In addition to these nine members of the teaching faculty—to which should be added President Phil Elliott, who taught courses in Milton and Shakespeare from time to time—Mrs. Dorothy Washburn Hamrick, Registrar, who became a member of the College staff in 1946, and Dr. W. Wyan Washburn, who taught journalism in the College from 1937-1940 and who came back as College physician in 1946, and Leonard Allen, custodian, should be listed with those who in the spring of 1956 had served the College for ten academic years or more.

From February 20 through February 24, 1956, the Baptist Student Union of the College sponsored a rather unique Religious Emphasis Week. This was not the first time the College had had a week of religious emphasis. Indeed, year in and year out, the Baptist Student Union had sponsored campus revival meetings or weeks designated as weeks of religious emphasis. This year, too, there was preaching in the mornings. However, following through with the over-all theme of "Partnership with God," a panel made up of Gardner-Webb faculty members discussed each evening some phase or aspect of the general theme. The students asked questions from the floor to the panelists on the stage in the E. B. Hamrick Auditorium. Here was something new. Professors W. F. Troutman, Jr., Robert A. Dyer, Robert N. Elliott, Jr., Vice-President W. Lawson Allen, and Dean J. O. Terrell discussed "Christian Attitudes in Race Relations." Professor S. L. Lamm, the Reverend John S. Farrar, Dean of Women Mabel Starnes, Mrs. John Lawrence, and Dean of Men J. Y. Hamrick considered student questions relating to "What Are My Moral Responsibilities as a Christian Student to My Fellowman and to My God?" On Wednesday evening, the theme "Which Should Come First, or What Emphasis Should Be Placed on the Religious, Social, and Intellectual Life?" was discussed by Registrar Dorothy W. Hamrick, Professors F. B. Dedmond, Paul Stacy, Laura Jean Keeter, and Mrs. Helen C. Barnett, Counselor for Girls. The next evening found Dean J. Y. Hamrick, Professors H. C. Dixon, R. A. Dyer, M. A. Moseley, Jr., and W. F. Troutman, Jr., considering "Christ in My Vocation." The Religious Emphasis Week, which had begun on Monday morning with a message by President Elliott entitled "Living in Time of Crisis" and which on the following mornings had included messages by students, was concluded on Friday morning when the Reverend H. Gordon Weekley, Jr., pastor of the Providence Baptist Church of Charlotte, N. C., preached on "A Vision Worth Following"—thus ending what may quite possibly become the prototype of the Religious Emphasis Weeks of the future on the Gardner-Webb campus.

Perhaps as the conclusion of this history, it would be fitting to quote a part of the final paragraph of President Phil Elliott's Report to the Trustees, dated May 26, 1956. President Elliott, in a division of his Report headed "Looking Ahead," mentioned the expected enrollment increase for the coming year, the projected Physical Education

Building and Science-Classroom Building, the thanks due the Board of Trustees "who are sympathetic, understanding, and loyal to the things we have set our hands to," the commendation due the faculty "for service beyond the line of duty," and so on. Then President Elliott added these words: "Finally, I should like to give thanks to our Heavenly Father, who has given us a task which challenges our best and which offers our best chance for extensive service. I hope with His help we shall erect here the truly Golden Temple to which the youth will come, many to find a new dedication to a higher citizenship than we have known."

FINIS

Appendices

Appendix A

CERTIFICATE OF INCORPORATION AND AMENDMENTS OF GARDNER-WEBB JUNIOR COLLEGE, INCORPORATED

STATE OF NORTH CAROLINA

S E A L

Department of State

To all to whom these presents shall come, Greeting:

I, Thad Eure, Secretary of State of the State of North Carolina, do hereby certify the following and hereto attached (TWENTY-FOUR (24) sheets) to be a true copy of

CERTIFICATE OF INCORPORATION AND AMENDMENTS

OF

GARDNER-WEBB JUNIOR COLLEGE, INCORPORATED

the original of which is now on file and a matter of record in this office.

In Witness Whereof, I have hereunto set my hand and affixed my official seal.

Done in Office, at Raleigh, this 22nd day of February in the year of our Lord 1949.

(Signed)   Thad Eure

Secretary of State

S E A L

CERTIFICATE OF INCORPORATION
OF THE
BOILING SPRINGS HIGH SCHOOL INCORPORATED.

This is to certify that we, the persons hereinafter named, do hereby associate ourselves into a corporation, under and by virtue of the provisions of an Act of the Legislature of the State of North Carolina (Session 1901), entitled "An act to revise the Corporation Law of North Carolina," and the several supplements thereto and acts amendatory thereof.

Article I. Corporate Name.

The name of the corporation is the "Boiling Springs High School, Incorporated."

Article II. Location of Office.

Sec. 1. The location of the office and place of business of said corporation is at Boiling Springs, No. 2 township, Cleveland County, North Carolina.

Sec. 2. The name of the agent therein and in charge thereof, upon whom process against this corporation may be served is Rev. J. V. Devenny, Chairman of the Board of Trustees, and his successor.

Article III. Object and Purpose.

Sec. 1. The objects for which this corporation is formed are to establish and maintain a school for the education of white children of both sexes at Boiling Springs, No. 2 township, Cleveland County, North Carolina; to provide a suitable building or buildings with all necessary furniture and appliances for the satisfactory conduct of said school; to employ teachers and fix their compensation, and to do all other things necessary and requisite for the maintenance of said school which shall afford scientific, literary, commercial and other educational training for those who shall avail themselves of the privileges of said school.

Sec. 2. This corporation shall have power to issue diplomas in a business or commercial department, and to issue certificates of proficiency in all other departments of said school.

Article IV. Capital Stock and Property.

Sec. 1. This shall be a non-stock corporation but said school shall be established and maintained by voluntary contributions and donations from the membership of the Kings Mountain and Sandy Run Baptist Associations, from such other persons as care to contribute, and from the income from said school.

Sec. 2. The said corporation shall have power to acquire by purchase, gift, or in any other way, property, real, personal or mixed, and may sell, exchange, mortgage, or otherwise dispose of its property and holdings.

Sec. 3. That said corporation shall not begin business till the subscriptions and donations, including all kinds of property, real, personal and mixed, shall amount to $5,000 in value, but shall be authorized to increase same from time to time till the limit of $25,000 is reached.

Article V. Trustees and Officers.

Sec. 1. This corporation shall be governed by a Board of Twenty-Five Trustees, fifteen (15) of whom shall be selected from and by the Kings Mountain Baptist Association, and ten (10) from and by the Sandy Run Baptist Association; said Trustees to be selected at such times and in such manner as said Associations shall elect, not inconsistent with the corporation law of this State.

Sec. 2. The officers of said Board of Trustees shall be a Chairman or President, a Secretary and a Treasurer who shall be elected at such times and in such manner as shall be provided for by the By-Laws of this Corporation.

Sec. 3.   The Board of Trustees of said school at its organization shall be as follows, and shall constitute the incorporators:

Name	Address
W. W. Washburn	Shelby, N. C., R.F.D. No. 4
J. E. McBrayer	Mooresboro, N. C.
A. H. Sims	Kings Mountain, N. C.
J. M. Wilson	Shelby, N. C., R.F.D. No. 5
J. V. Devenny	Shelby, N. C., R.F.D. No. 3
E. C. Borders	Shelby, N. C., R.F.D. No. 2
J. H. Quinn	Shelby, N. C.
R. L. Weathers	Shelby, N. C., R.F.D. No. 5
G. H. Logan	Crocker, N. C.
A. C. Irvin	Shelby, N. C., R.F.D. No. 5
Carme Elam	Lawndale, N. C.
E. B. Hamrick	Shelby, N. C., R.F.D. No. 3
N. B. Kendrick	Cherryville, N. C.
L. S. Hamrick	Shelby, N. C., R.F.D. No. 4
Jno. F. Moore	Mooresboro, N. C., R.F.D. No. 2
T. G. Hamrick	Caroleen, N. C.
J. J. Edwards	Ellenboro, N. C., R.F.D. No. 2
T. M. Holland	Ellenboro, N. C., R.F.D. No. 1
J. F. Alexander	Forest City, N. C.
W. A. Martin	Mooresboro, N. C.
A. S. Harrill	Ellenboro, N. C.
J. C. Bridges	Ellenboro, N. C., R.F.D. No. 2
D. M. Harrill	Ellenboro, N. C., R.F.D. No. 2
J. H. Hamrick	Cliffside, N. C.
T. B. Lovelace	Henrietta, N. C.

Sec. 4.   The following shall be the officers of said Board at its organization: Chairman, Rev. J. V. Devenny; Secretary, Carme Elam; and Treasurer, W. A. Martin, who shall hold office until their successors are elected.

Article VI.   Duration.

The period of existence of this corporation is unlimited.

Article VII.   By-Laws.

It shall be the duty of said Trustees at their first meeting after becoming a body corporate, to adopt By-Laws for the proper execution of the purposes for which it is organized.

In Witness whereof, we have hereunto set our hands and seals this the 13th day of November, 1905.

J. V. Devenny	(SEAL)
Carme Elam	(SEAL)
J. H. Quinn	(SEAL)
A. C. Irvin	(SEAL)
L. S. Hamrick	(SEAL)
R. L. Weathers	(SEAL)
T. M. Holland	(SEAL)
W. W. Washburn	(SEAL)
J. F. Moore	(SEAL)
T. G. Hamrick	(SEAL)
J. H. Hamrick	(SEAL)
E. B. Hamrick	(SEAL)
W. A. Martin	(SEAL)

NORTH CAROLINA
                          SS
CLEVELAND COUNTY

Be it remembered that on this 13th day of November A. D. 1905, before me a Justice of the Peace in and for said county, personally appeared J. V. Devenny, Carme Elam, J. H. Quinn, A. C. Irvin, L. S. Hamrick, R. L. Weathers, T. M. Holland, W. W. Washburn, J. F. Moore, T. G. Hamrick, J. H. Hamrick, E. B. Hamrick, and W. A. Martin, who, I am satisfied are the persons named in and who executed the foregoing certificate of incorporation, and I having first made known to them the contents thereof, they did each acknowledge that they signed, sealed and delivered the same as their own voluntary act and deed for the uses and purposes therein expressed.

                                        J. B. Hamrick, J.P.

NORTH CAROLINA,
CLEVELAND COUNTY.

I, L. J. Hoyle, Clerk Superior Court, Cleveland County, do hereby certify that J. B. Hamrick was at the time of the signing of the foregoing certificate an acting Justice of the Peace in and for the county of Cleveland and State of North Carolina and that his signature thereto is in his own proper handwriting.

In Witness whereof I hereby set my hand and official seal, this the 29th day of November, 1905.

                                        L. J. Hoyle
                                        Clerk Superior Court,
                                        Cleveland County.

(OFFICIAL SEAL)

Certificate of Incorporation of "Boiling Springs High School, Incorporated," filed the 1st day of December, 1905.

....
                              Secretary of State

                    FILED DEC 2 1905
                    J. BRYAN GRIMES
                    SECRETARY OF STATE

CERTIFICATE OF AMENDMENT OF THE CHARTER
BOILING SPRINGS HIGH SCHOOL, INC.

The location of the principal office in this State is in the Main School Building, in the town of Boiling Springs, County of Cleveland. The name of the agent therein and in charge thereof, upon whom process against this corporation may be served, is E. B. Hamrick.

RESOLUTIONS OF TRUSTEES

The Board of Trustees of the "Boiling Springs High School, Incorporated," a corporation created and existing under the laws of North Carolina, in a meeting duly called and held on this the 16th day of December, 1921, do hereby resolve and declare that it is advisable that the Charter of said School be amended as follows, to-wit:
1. That Section 2 of Article II, be amended by striking out in line three the words "Rev. J. V. Devenny, Chairman," and by inserting in lieu thereof the words "E. B. Hamrick, Treasurer."
II. That Section 2 of Article III. be amended by striking out all words in the paragraph, following the word "diplomas," and inserting in lieu thereof the words "or certificates of proficiency in all departments of the School."
III. That Section 1 of Article IV. be amended by inserting in line four thereof, after the word "Run" and before the word "Baptist," the following words: "and Gaston County."
IV. That all of Section 3 of Article IV. be stricken out and the following section inserted in lieu thereof: "Sec. 3. That this corporation shall have the right to have and to hold an unlimited amount of property—real, personal and mixed."
V. That Section 1 of Article V. be amended by striking out in line two the words "twenty-five" and inserting in lieu thereof the words, "thirty-five (35)" and by inserting at the end of line four, after the word "Association" and before the semicolon (;), the words "and ten (10) from and by the Gaston County Baptist Association," and by adding at the end of said paragraph the following sentence: "That the following shall constitute the members of said Board from the Gaston County Association until their successors are duly elected by the Gaston County Association, to-wit: Rev. W. C. Barrett, Dr. J. L. Vipperman, Rev. C. J. Black, Rev. T. H. King, Rev. D. F. Putnam, N. B. Kendrick, W. J. Francis, A. U. Stroup, R. F. Craig and J. E. C. Ford."
VI. That all of Sec. 4 of Article V. be stricken out as obsolete.
That a meeting of the Board of Trustees of the "Boiling Springs High School, Inc." is hereby called to meet at the Royster Building in Shelby, N. C., on the 2nd day of January, 1922, to take action upon the foregoing resolutions.

CERTIFICATE OF CHANGE

The "Boiling Springs High School, Inc.", a corporation of the State of North Carolina, doth hereby certify that it has unanimously adopted the following resolution through a special meeting of its Board of Trustees duly called and held on this the 2nd day of January, 1922, for this purpose, to-wit:
"Resolved, that the recommendations of the Board of Trustees of "Boiling Springs High School, Inc.", as contained in a series of six (6) resolutions adopted by said Board of Trustees at a special meeting regularly called and held on the 16th day of December, 1921, relative to

amendment of Charter of said School, be and same are hereby approved and adopted to the end that said Charter be amended accordingly," said amendments having been declared by resolutions of the Board of Trustees of said School, as appear under the sub-head, "Resolutions of Trustees," above, to be advisable, and having been duly and regularly assented to by the vote of two-thirds of the members of the Board of Trustees of said School, at a meeting duly called by the said Board for the purpose; and the written assent of said Trustees is hereto appended.

In Witness whereof, said corporation has caused this certificate to be signed by the Chairman of its Board of Trustees and its Secretary, and its corporate seal to be hereto affixed, the 2nd day of January, A. D., 1922.

> Boiling Springs High School, Inc.
> By J. H. Quinn,
> Chairman Board Trustees.

Attest: G. B. Pruette
          Secretary Board Trustees

(CORPORATE SEAL)

STATE OF NORTH CAROLINA,
                                        SS.
COUNTY OF CLEVELAND.

Be it remembered that on this 2nd day of January, A. D., 1922, before me, the subscriber, a Notary Public, personally appeared G. B. Pruette, Secretary of the Board of Trustees of Boiling Springs High School, Inc., the corporation mentioned in and which executed the foregoing certificate, who, being by me duly sworn on his oath says that he is such secretary, and that the seal affixed to said certificate is the corporate seal of said corporation, the same being well known to him; that J. H. Quinn is Chairman of the Board of Trustees of said corporation, and signed said certificate by authority of the Board of Trustees, and with the assent of at least two-thirds of the members of the Board of Trustees of said corporation, as and for his voluntary act and deed, and the voluntary act and deed of said corporation in presence of deponent, who thereupon subscribed his name thereto as witness.

And he further says that the assent hereto appended is signed by at least two-thirds of the members of the Board of Trustees of said corporation in persons.

> H. T. Bess
> Notary Public.

(NOTARIAL SEAL)

(My commission expires 1/26/22)

TRUSTEES' ASSENT TO CHANGES

We, the undersigned, being more than two-thirds of all of the Trustees of Boiling Springs High School, Incorporated, having at a meeting regularly called for the purpose of amending the charter of said corporation voted in favor of amending the charter of said corporation, as set forth in the certificate of the officers of said corporation hereto attached, do now, pursuant to the statute hereby give our written assent to the said changes.

Witness our hand this 2nd day of January, 1922.

J. II. Quinn
G. B. Pruette
E. B. Hamrick
J. W. Suttle
B. T. Falls
D. F. Hord
C. D. Forney
W. K. Collins
A. I. Jolley

A. D. Lancaster
D. M. Harrill
D. J. Hunt
Z. R. Walter
J. J. Edwards
T. M. Holland
M. M. Greene
W. W. Washburn
A. E. Bettis

FILED JAN 9 1922
J. BRYAN GRIMES,
SECRETARY OF STATE

CERTIFICATE OF AMENDMENT
OF
CERTIFICATE OF INCORPORATION

Boiling Springs High School, Incorporated, a corporation organized under and by virtue of the provisions of an act of the Legislature of the State of North Carolina (Session 1901) entitled, "An act to revise the Corporation Law of North Carolina," and the several supplements thereto and acts amendatory thereof, the Certificate of Incorporation of which was filed in the office of the Secretary of State for the State of North Carolina on December 2, 1905, and a certified copy thereof duly filed in the office of the Clerk of the Superior Court for Cleveland County, State of North Carolina, and an amendment to the Certificate of Incorporation of which was filed in the office of the Secretary of State for the State of North Carolina on January 9, 1922, and a certified copy thereof duly filed in the office of the Clerk of the Superior Court for Cleveland County, State of North Carolina, does hereby certify:

First: That at a meeting of the Board of Trustees of said Corporation, duly held and convened, resolutions were duly adopted setting forth proposed amendments to the Certificate of Incorporation of said Corporation and declaring said amendments advisable and calling a meeting of the Board of Trustees for consideration thereof. The resolutions setting forth the proposed amendments are, as follows:

Resolved that the Certificate of Incorporation of this Corporation be amended by changing the Preamble thereof to read as follows:

This is to certify that we, the persons hereinafter named, do hereby associate ourselves into a non-stock, non-profit corporation, under and by virtue of the provisions of an act of the Legislature of the State of North Carolina (Session 1901) entitled "An act to revise the Corporation Law of North Carolina," and the several supplements thereto and acts amendatory thereof.

Further Resolved that the Certificate of Incorporation of this Corporation be amended by striking out Article I thereof and substituting therefor the following:

ARTICLE I

The name of this Corporation is the Gardner-Webb Junior College, Incorporated.

Further Resolved that the Certificate of Incorporation of this Corporation be amended by striking out Article II thereof and substituting therefor the following:

ARTICLE II

The office and principal place of business of this Corporation is located at the Main School Building, in the Town of Boiling Springs, County of Cleveland.

Further Resolved that the Certificate of Incorporation of this Corporation be amended by striking out Article III thereof and substituting therefor the following:

ARTICLE III

The objects for which this Corporation is formed are:

Section 1. To establish and maintain a school and junior college in the Town of Boiling Springs, County of Cleveland, at which liberal arts, literary, scientific, commercial, vocational (including textile, agricultural, machine shop, etc.) and other additional training shall be afforded to those white persons of both sexes who shall avail themselves of the privileges of said college; to provide a suitable building or buildings with all necessary furniture and appliances for the satisfactory conduct of said college; to employ teachers and fix their compensation; to issue diplomas or certificates of proficiency in all departments of said college; and, in general, to do all things necessary for the maintenance, progress and development of said college;

Section 2. To borrow money and secure the same, to solicit, receive and acquire, by grant, gift, purchase, devise, bequest, or otherwise, money and property of every type, kind, nature and description, and to administer, sell, exchange, mortgage, or otherwise dispose of and use the money and property of this Corporation and any and all income derived therefrom for any one or more of the purposes specified in this Article III; and

Section 3. To do any and all things necessary, suitable, convenient or proper in connection with, or incidental to, the accomplishment of any of the purposes specified in this Article III; and, in general, to do any and all things, and to exercise any and all powers, in furtherance of any one or more of the purposes specified in this Article III which it may now or hereafter be lawful for this Corporation to do or exercise under the laws of the State of North Carolina that may now or hereafter be applicable to this Corporation.

This Corporation is not organized for pecuniary profit, and shall have no power to issue certificates of stock or to make or declare dividends. No part of the net earnings of this Corporation shall inure to the benefit of any member of this Corporation or any other individual.

Further Resolved that the Certificate of Incorporation of this Corporation be amended by striking out Article IV thereof and substituting the following:

ARTICLE IV

This Corporation shall have no capital stock. The school and junior College, which it is the purpose of this Corporation to establish and maintain, shall be supported by voluntary contributions from such persons, corporations, and associations a may care to contribute and by use of the income from said school and junior college.

Further Resolved that the Certificate of Incorporation of this Corporation be amended by renumbering Section 3 of Article V as Section 4 of Article V, and by renumbering Section 4 of Article V as Section 5 of Article V, and by striking out Sections 1 and 2 of Article V and substituting therefor the following three (3) sections:

ARTICLE V

Section 1. The Board of Trustees of this Corporation shall be composed of fifty (50) members. The members of the Board of Trustees at the time of the taking effect of this Amendment to the Certificate of Incorporation, fifteen (15) of whom have been elected by the Kings Mountain Baptist Association and ten (10) of whom have been elected by the Sandy Run Baptist Association, shall hold office until June 1, 1944, and until their successors are duly elected and qualified in the manner hereinafter specified. The remaining twenty-five (25) members of the Board of Trustees shall be elected by the other members of the Board of Trustees in such a manner that the terms of office of nine (9) of such number of twenty-five (25) members shall be for one (1) year, and until their successors are duly elected and qualified, the terms of office of eight (8) of such number of twenty-five (25) members shall be for two (2) years, and until their successors are duly elected and qualified, and the terms of office of eight (8) of such number of twenty-five (25) members shall be for three (3) years, and until their successors are duly elected and qualified.

Fifteen (15) of the successors to the twenty-five (25) members of the Board of Trustees, whose terms of office expire on June 1, 1944, shall be chosen by the Kings Mountain Baptist Association in such a manner that the terms of office of five (5) shall be for one (1) year, and until their successors are duly elected and qualified, the terms of office of five (5) shall be for two (2) years, and until their successors are duly elected and qualified, and the terms of office of five (5) shall be for three (3) years, and until their successors are duly elected and qualified, and ten (10) of the successors to the twenty-five (25) members of the Board of Trustees whose terms of office expire on June 1, 1944, shall be chosen by the Sandy Run Baptist Association in such a manner that the terms of office of four (4) shall be for one (1) year, and until their successors are duly elected and qualified, the terms of office of three (3) shall be for two (2) years, and until their successors are duly elected and qualified, and the terms of office of three (3) shall be for three (3) years, and until their successors are duly elected and qualified.

If any vacancy occurs in the membership of the Board of Trustees by reason of the death, resignation, withdrawal or disqualification of any Trustee, the Board of Trustess shall elect a new Trustee who shall hold office for the unexpired term of the Trustee thus replaced, and until his successor has been elected and qualified.

Except for the filling of vacancies in the membership of the Board of Trustees, which is provided for in the immediately preceding paragraph of this Section 1 of Article V, it is the purpose of this Section 1 of Article V to provide for the election of one-half of the membership of the Board of Trustees by the Kings Mountain and Sandy Run Baptist Associations, in the manner hereinbefore specified, and to provide for the election of the remaining one-half of the membership of the Board of Trustees by the Board of Trustees itself, in the manner hereinbefore specified

Section 2. The Board of Trustees shall elect from among its membership a Chairman who shall hold office until his successor is duly elected and qualified.

Section 3. The Trustees shall have power to appoint, or may give the Chairman of the Board of Trustees power to appoint, from among the membership of the Board of Trustees, an Executive Committee of not more than nine (9) or less than six (6) members which shall be clothed with such powers as the Trustees shall confer.

Further Resolved that the Certificate of Incorporation of this Corporation be amended by adding thereto the following Article VIII:

ARTICLE VIII

The officers of this Corporation shall be a Chairman of the Board of Trustees, a President, a Secretary, and a Treasurer, who shall be elected at such times and in such manner as shall be provided for in the By-Laws of this Corporation.

Second: That thereafter, upon notice duly given, a meeting of the Board of Trustees was held and the foregoing Resolutions were duly and legally assented to by the vote of two-thirds of the Board of Trustees of this Corporation, whose written assents are hereto appended.

Third: That said Amendments to the Certificate of Incorporation of this Corporation were duly adopted in accordance with the provisions of Section 1132 of the North Carolina Code of 1935.

In Witness Whereof, said Boiling Springs High School, Incorporated, has caused its corporate seal to be hereunto affixed and this Certificate

to be signed by E. Y. Webb, Chairman of its Board of Trustees, and by
W. L. Hicks, its Secretary, this 22 day of Aug., 1942.

> Boiling Springs High School, Incorporated
> By E. Y. Webb
> Chairman of Board of Trustees

(CORPORATE SEAL)   By W. L. Hicks
                                    Secretary

We, the undersigned, being more than two-thirds of all the Trustees
of Boiling Springs High School, Incorporated, having voted, at a meeting
duly and legally held, in favor of amending the charter of said Corporation as set forth in the Certificate of the officers of said Corporation
hereto attached, do now, pursuant to the statute in such cases made and
provided, give our written assent to said changes.

Witness our hands this 22 day of August, 1942.

J. W. Suttle	J. C. Washburn
M. A. Spangler	J. U. Rollins
A. W. McMurry	Mrs. John Wacaster
G. V. Hawkins	Mrs. Rush Stroup
Lester O. Hamrick	Horace Easom
A. V. Hamrick	W. L. Hicks
O. Max Gardner	C. E. Hamrick
Joe Lee Woodward	J. F. Lutz
Mrs. Norman B. Lee	Mrs. E. G. Spurling
Ernest W. Bailes	A. G. Sargeant
W. H. Hudson	E. Y. Webb
W. V. Tarlton	

STATE OF NORTH CAROLINA
                                    SS.
COUNTY OF CLEVELAND

Be It Remembered, that on the 1 day of Aug., 1942, personally came
before me, Stephen Woodson, a notary public in and for the county and
state aforesaid, W. L. Hicks, Secretary of Boiling Springs High School,
Incorporated, a corporation of the State of North Carolina, which is
the Corporation described in and which executed the foregoing Certificate, and is known to me personally to be such; and he, the said W. L.
Hicks, as such Secretary, before me duly acknowledged that the signatures of the Chairman of the Board of Trustees and of the said Secretary
of said Corporation to said foregoing Certificate are in the handwriting
of the said Chairman and said Secretary of said Corporation, respectively,
that the seal affixed to the said Certificate is the corporate seal of said
Corporation, that his act of sealing, executing, acknowledging and delivering the said Certificate, and the similar acts of the Chairman, were
duly authorized by the Board of Trustees of said Corporation, that the
said Certificate is his voluntary act and deed and the voluntary act and
deed of said Corporation, and that the assent hereto appended is signed
by at least two-thirds of the members of the Board of Trustees of said
Corporation.

In Witness Whereof I have hereunto set my hand and seal of office
the day and year first above stated.

> Stephen Woodson
(NOTARIAL SEAL)   Notary Public

My Commission expires Jan. 12, 1943
                  FILED AUG 27 1942
                  THAD EURE
                  SECRETARY OF STATE

GARDNER-WEBB JUNIOR COLLEGE, INCORPORATED
CERTIFICATE OF AMENDMENT
OF
CERTIFICATE OF INCORPORATION

Boiling Springs High School, Incorporated, a corporation organized under and by virtue of the provisions of an act of the Legislature of the State of North Carolina (Session 1901) entitled "An act to revise the Corporation Law of North Carolina", and the several supplements thereto and acts amendatory thereof, the certificate of incorporation of which was filed in the office of the Secretary of State for the State of North Carolina on December 2, 1905, and a certified copy thereof duly filed in the office of the Clerk of the Superior Court for Cleveland County, State of North Carolina, and an amendment to the certificate of incorporation of which was filed in the office of the Secretary of State for the State of North Carolina on January 9, 1922, and a certified copy thereof duly filed in the office of the Clerk of the Superior Court for Cleveland County, State of North Carolina, and a further amendment to the certificate of incorporation which was filed in the office of the Secretary of State of North Carolina on August 27, 1942, a certified copy thereof duly filed in the office of the Clerk of Superior Court of Cleveland County, State of North Carolina, does hereby certify:

That at a meeting of the Board of Trustees of said corporation, duly held, it was ordered, by unanimous vote, that its amended certificate of incorporation be further amended as follows:

Be it resolved that the amended certificate of incorporation of this corporation be amended by striking out Section 1 of Article V and by inserting in lieu thereof the following:

ARTICLE V

Section 1. The Board of Trustees of Gardner-Webb Junior College, Incorporated, shall be composed of not less than 20 nor more than 40 members who shall be elected by the Baptist State Convention of North Carolina and their regular term of office shall be for four years.

a. At the first election by the Convention one-fourth of the board of trustees shall be elected to serve for one year, one-fourth for two years, one-fourth for three years, and the remaining one-fourth for four years. At each subsequent regular annual session of the Baptist State Convention of North Carolina one-fourth of the members of the Board of Trustees of said corporation shall be elected by the Convention to succeed the members of said Board retiring, the retiring members being ineligible for re-election until one year has elapsed.

b. The members of the Board of Trustees of said corporation shall be residents of the State of North Carolina and members in good and regular standing of a Missionary Baptist Church co-operating with the Baptist State Convention of North Carolina.

c. Removal from the State or ceasing for any reason to be a member in good and regular standing of a Missionary Baptist Church co-operating with the Baptist State Convention of North Carolina shall be equivalent to a resignation from said Board of Trustees. Any vacancy on the Board shall be filled by the remaining members until the next regular annual session of the Convention and the Convention shall at its next regular session fill the vacancy for the unexpired term.

d. The term of office of a trustee who has not resigned, died, become disqualified, or been removed shall not expire until his successor shall have been duly elected and qualified.

e. The Board of Trustees of said corporation by the affirmative vote of three-fourths of its entire membership given in regular annual meeting or in a special meeting duly called for the purpose, shall have power to remove from office any trustee of such corporation for cause considered sufficient by such Board, but only after reasonable notice to such trustee and opportunity to him to be heard by the Board.

f. The Baptist State Convention shall have the right at any time to remove from office any trustee for cause considered sufficient by the Convention, but only after reasonable notice to such trustee and opportunity for him to be heard by the Convention. Notice of such contemplated action and hearing by the Convention may be given by the Executive Committee of the Convention.

g. That no individual shall serve on any Board or Institution, who is at the time holding membership on any other Board or Institution.

That thereafter, upon notice duly given, a meeting of the Board of Trustees was held and the foregoing Resolutions were duly and legally assented to by the vote of two-thirds of the Board of Trustees of this corporation, whose written assents are hereto appended.

That said amendment to the certificate of incorporation of this corporation was duly adopted in accordance with the provisions of Section 1132 of the North Carolina Code of 1935.

In witness whereof, said Gardner-Webb Junior College, Incorporated, has caused its corporate seal to be hereunto affixed and this certificate to be signed by E. Y. Webb, Chairman of its Board of Trustees, and by W. L. Hicks, its Secretary, this 23rd day of October, 1946.

> GARDNER-WEBB JUNIOR COLLEGE,
> INCORPORATED
> By E. Y. Webb
> Chairman of Board of Trustees
> W. L. Hicks
> Secretary

(CORPORATE SEAL)

We, the undersigned, being more than two-thirds of all the Trustees of Gardner-Webb College, Incorporated, having voted, at a meeting duly and legally held, in favor of the certificate of incorporation as set forth in the certificate of the officers of said corporation hereto attached, do now, pursuant to the statute in such cases made and provided, give our written assent to said changes.

Witness our hand this 23rd day of Oct., 1946.

O. M. Mull	C. E. Hamrick
Zeno Wall	Selma C. Webb
A. V. Hamrick	Lester O. Hamrick
C. Rush Hamrick	J. C. Washburn
Horace Easom	E. A. Hamrick
J. W. Suttle	W. H. Hudson
Mrs. Rush Stroup	O. Max Gardner, Jr.
A. V. McMurry	O. Max Gardner, Sr.
J. U. Rollins	G. H. Roberts
W. L. Hicks	T. T. Long
G. V. Hawkins	Margaret Young
M. A. Spangler	Mrs. T. R. Padgett
Yates Smith	(Rev.) M. D. Blanton
W. E. Pettit	R. E. Price
J. J. Tarlton	

STATE OF NORTH CAROLINA

                                    ss.

COUNTY OF CLEVELAND,

Be it remembered, that on the 23rd day of Oct., 1946, personally came before me, Leonard Allen, a notary public in and for the county and state aforesaid, W. L. Hicks, Secretary of Gardner-Webb Junior College, Incorporated, a corporation of the State of North Carolina, which is the corporation described in and which executed the foregoing certificate, and is known to me personally to be such; and he, the said W. L. Hicks, as such Secretary, before me duly acknowledged that the signatures of the Chairman of the Board of Trustees and of the said Secretary of said corporation to said foregoing certificate are in the handwriting of the said Chairman and said Secretary of said corporation, respectively, that the seal affixed to the said certificate is the corporate seal of said corporation, that his act of sealing, executing, acknowledging and delivering the said certificate, and the similar acts of the Chairman, were duly authorized by the Board of Trustees of said corporation, that the said certificate is his voluntary act and deed and the voluntary act and deed of said corporation, and that the assent hereto appended is signed by at least two-thirds of the members of the Board of Trustees of said corporation.

In witness whereof I have hereunto set my hand and seal of office the day and year first above stated.

                              Leonard A. Allen
                              Notary Public

(NOTARIAL SEAL)

My commission expires Oct. 18, 1947
Sworn to and subscribed before me this 23
day of October, 1946. Witness my hand
and official seal

(Signed)   Leonard A. Allen
           Notary Public

              FILED MAR 6 1947

              THAD EURE
              SECRETARY OF STATE

Appendix B

FACULTY AND ADMINISTRATIVE PERSONNEL
FROM 1907-08 THROUGH 1955-56

Name	Office	Degree	Subject Taught	Year
Ables, Mary E.		B.S.; M.A.	English; Education	1930-34
Allen, Leonard Ancel	Business Manager; Custodian			1945-56
Allen, William Lawson	Director of Public Relations; Acting President; Vice-President	B.S.; M.R.E.	Religious Education	1944-46; 1953-56
Amis, Thelma Agnes (See Mrs. Carroll Raines)				
Arnette, J. M.		A.B.	Bible; Greek; Latin	1928-33
Arnette, Josephine		B.M.	Voice	1934-35
Baldwin, Willie Kate	Dean of Women	B.A.; M.R.E.	English	1949-50
Banks, Etta		A.B.	Household Arts; Expression	1918-22
Barbee, Cornelia H.	Assistant to Dean of Women; Assistant Librarian	B.S.		1911-13
Barnett, Mrs. Helen C.			Director of Music	1952-56
Barnhill, Frances	Librarian	A.B.		1929-32
Bell, George Alexander		A.B.	Modern Language	1932-36
Black, Mrs. Jessie Wade		B.S.	Home Economics	1946-47
Blanton, F. Y.			Commercial	1917-19
Brown, F. A.	Joint-Principal	B.S.	Science; History; Mathematics	1908-10
Brown, Katherine M.		B.S.	Physical Education	1942-43
Brown, Mrs. M. J.	Matron			1909-10
Bostick, Adelaide P.	Counselor for Girls	A.B.; A.M.	English; Psychology	1936-39
Bradburn, Charles Wayne	Coach	B.S.; M.S.	Physical Education; Health	1946-52
Burnett, Frances George		A.B.	English; Speech	1937-38
Burnett, George J.	President	A.B.; A.M.		1936-39

FACULTY AND ADMINISTRATIVE PERSONNEL (cont'd)

Name	Office	Degree	Subject Taught	Year
Burnett, Laura Yates		A.B.	Speech	1936-39
Cade, Rev. Baylus			History; Bible	1908-10
Canaday, Flora B.		B.M.	Music	1930-32
Cantrell, John Roland	President	A.B.	Bible	1939-43
Carr, Noel Cleveland		A.B.; M.A.; M.E.	Physics; Mathematics	1947-48
Carr, Robert George		B.M.; M.M.	Music; French	1954-56
Carson, Mrs. Nellie Poole	Dietitian			1954-55
Clark, Monta J.		Diploma in Art	Art; China Painting; French	1925-27
Copeland, Kathryn		A.B.; B.M.T.; M.A.	English	1954-56
Cornwell, Mrs. Carlyle		B.S.; M.S.	Home Economics	1949-50
Crawley, Dr. Sam J., Jr.	College Physician	B.S.; M.D.		1953-56
Crisp, Marjorie	Dean of Women	B.S.	Physical Education	1935-42
Curtis, Etta L.	Dean of Women; Bookkeeper		Intermediate Dept.	1909-36
Cuthbertson, Frances A.	Dean of Women	B.A.; M.A.	English; Dramatics	1940-49
Davidson, Mrs. Elma Hersley		B.M.T.	High School	1938-41
Davidson, William W.		A.B.; Th.M.	Bible; Psychology; Greek	1939-45
Davis, Mrs. Jackie Parker	Dietitian			1954 (Spring)
Davis, James Blaine	President	M.A.; Th.M.	Bible; Mathematics	1928-30
Davis, Kathleen Holt	Secretary	B.S.	English; Commercial	1952-56
Dedmond, Francis B.	Head, Department of English	A.B.; Th.M.; M.A.	English	1952-56
DeShong, Jessie Franklin	Librarian	B.S.; B.S.L.S.		1954-56
Dixon, Hubert Conrad	Dean; Registrar; Vice-President	B.A.; M.A.	Mathematics	1935-44; 1946-56
Dixon, Mrs. Hubert Conrad	Registrar; Director of Religious Activities	B.Mus.	Music	1933-36; 1940-45

FACULTY AND ADMINISTRATIVE PERSONNEL (cont'd)

Name	Office	Degree	Subject Taught	Year
Dodson, Myrtle Louise		B.M.	Music	1908-11
Dover, Margaret			Assistant in Music	1918-19
Downer, Harriette	Dean of Women	A.B.	Voice	1938-41
Dyer, Robert Allen	Director of Guidance	B.A.; Th.M.; Th.D.	Bible; Psychology	1946-56
Dyer, Mrs. Robert Allen		B.M.	Voice	1950-53
Elliott, Philip Lovin	President	B.A.; M.A.; Ed.D.	English	1943-56
Elliott, Robert N., Jr.		B.S.; M.A.; Ph.D.	Social Science	1953-56
Elliott, Mrs. Robert N.		A.B.	English	1954-55
English, Gwendolen			English	1910-12
Fales, Margaret		B.M.	Organ	1949-50
Farris, T. N.			Commerce	1908-10
Fisher, Benjamin Coleman	Executive Assistant to President	A.B.; B.D.	English	1947-53
Fisher, Mrs. Benjamin Coleman		A.B.; M.A.	English	1950-52
Foster, Sarah L.		A.B.	Latin	1922-25
Francis, Hester			Commercial; Intermediate Dept.	1912-14
Francis William J.	Principal	A.B.	Bible	1911-14
Frye, Revis	Coach	B.S.; M.S.	Physical Education; Health; Radio	1947-49
Fuller, Bettsy Jane		B.A.	Voice	1944-45
Gamble, Emmalyn		B.M.	Voice	1947-50
Garrison, Carolyn		B.S.	Household Arts and Science	1924-28
Garrison, James Gardner	Assistant Coach	B.S.	Physical Education; Health; Mathematics	1955-56
Gary, W. Kays		B.A.	Journalism	1947-48

FACULTY AND ADMINISTRATIVE PERSONNEL (cont'd)

Name	Office	Degree	Subject Taught	Year
Gidney, Mrs. Robert Sarratt		B.M.	Voice	1945-47; 1953-56
Greene, Mrs. Hal B.	Dietitian			1947-48
Greene, William L., Jr.		A.B.	Journalism	Fall 1955
Goode, Velma	Librarian	A.B.	Commercial	1936-43
Griffin, I. C.			Education	1920-21
Hammett, H. G.		B.A.	English; Mathematics	1926-29
Hamrick, A. Franklin		B.A.; M.A.	Social Science	1934-36
Hamrick, Ada		B.A.	High School	1929-35
Hamrick, Annie		B.L.	Preparatory Dept.	1907-08; 1909-11
Hamrick, Dorothy W.	Registrar	B.A.		1946-56
Hamrick, Elijah B.	Bursar			1909-10
Hamrick, Eunice				1953-56
Hamrick, Euzelia	Nurse	R.N.		1910-19
Hamrick, Mrs. F. B.		B.L.	Latin; History	1919-21; 1922-24
Hamrick, J. M.	Principal		Assistant in Music	1910-12
Hamrick, James Young	Dean of Men	B.A.; M.A.	Bible	1945-56
Hamrick, Julian W.	Bursar	B.S.	English; Band; Dramatics	1953-56
Hamrick, Marietta		B.A.	Biology	1948-50
Hamrick, O. P.	Bursar	A.B.	English; Education	1914-36
Hamrick, Mrs. O. P.			Domestic Science; Art; China Painting; Expression	1916-17; 1918-19
				1922-25
Hamrick, Sadie		A.B; M.A.	Business Administration	1947-48
Hamrick, Sarah Lee		B.A.	High School	1933-35

FACULTY AND ADMINISTRATIVE PERSONNEL (cont'd)

Name	Office	Subject Taught	Degree	Year
Harper, Elma Estelle (See Mrs. John Mark Pollock)				
Harrill, Clive V.		Science	B.A.; M.A.	1934-35
Harris, Mrs. Dana H.		Social Science; English	A.B.; M.A.; M.A.	1950-54
Harris, Mrs. James Nesbitt	Dietitian	Home Economics	B.A.	1944-45
Harris, Mary Ella		English; Mathematics	A.B.	1925-26
Harris, Norman	Coach	Physical Education, Health	B.A.; M.S.	1949-56
Harris, Mrs. Norman		Typing		Fall 1949
Hathcock, Myrna		Physical Education	B.S.	1942-43
Haynes, Mrs. Charles		Physical Education; Health	B.S.	1955-56
Hendricks, Garland A.		Church-Community Development	A.B.; Th.B.	1950-53
Hendricks, Paul E.		Band Instructor	B.S.	1937-39
Hicks, Walter L.	Business Manager			1931-32; 1933-34
Highsmith, Eunice	Nurse		R.N.	1945-47
Hill, Annie L.		Home Economics	B.S.	1942-44
Hill, Frank P.		Science	B.S.; M.A.	1930-32
Holland, Griffin			A.B.	1941-42
Holland, T. C.	Dean of Men	Spanish; Bible; Latin	A.B.; M.A.; Th.D.	1915-17; 1945-46
Honeycutt, Mrs. H. H.		Expression; Art		1929-30; 1931-33
Huggins, James Dwyre, Sr.	Principal of High School; Dean of College	Mathematics; Science; Elocution	A.B.	1907-29; 1930-32
Huggins, Mrs. James Dwyre, Sr.	Counselor for Girls	English; Latin	A.B.	1908-10; 1911-16; 1925-29; 1930-31; 1945-52
Hughes, S. M.		Greek; Bible	B.S.; B.D.	1955-56

FACULTY AND ADMINISTRATIVE PERSONNEL (cont'd)

Name	Office	Degree	Subject Taught	Year
Hullender, R. E.			Commercial	1919-21
Hutchins, Paul W.	Coach	B.S.; M.A.	Physical Education	1932-34
Inman, Sarah Elizabeth		A.B.; A.M.	English	1939-40
James, Margaret L.		B.S.; B.M.	Music	1936-38
Jenkins, James L.	President	A.B.	Bible; Religion	1928-29; 1932-35; 1937-45
Jenks, Tilli Ann		A.B.	Voice; Public School Music	1935-36
Jessup, Martha Louis		B.S.M.	Voice	1941-44
Johnson, Mrs. J. F.	House Counselor			1933-36
Johnson, Lucile				
(See Mrs. Hubert Conrad Dixon)				
Jolley, A. I.	Business Manager			1933-34; 1935-36
Jolley, Evelyn	Librarian	A.B.	Mathematics; English	1934-36
Jones, Dorothy		B.A.	Organ	1951-52
Jones, Rachel Agnes			Assistant in Music	1923-26
Jolley, Mrs. Tom	Nurse	R.N.		1947-53
Jordan, J. Karl		B.A.	Voice; Public School Music	1931-33
Keeter, Laura Jean		B.S.	French; Commercial Scouting	1954-56
Kennedy, Paul				1948-49
Kneece, Eunice E.	Dean of Women	B.A.	History; French; English	1927-30; 1931-33
Kirby, Rosa	Matron			1910-15
Lamm, S. L.		B.A.; Th.M.	Bible; Speech	1950-56
Lawhon, Edgar A.	Coach	B.A.	Physical Education	1934-36
Lawrence, Lois			Assistant in Music	1924-27
Lee, Mary Pettigrew		B.Mus.	Music	1932-34

FACULTY AND ADMINISTRATIVE PERSONNEL (cont'd)

Name	Office	Degree	Subject Taught	Year
Lee, Ralph M.		A.B.	Science; Bible	1922-23
Lewis, Ovid B.			Violin, Cello, Wind Instruments	1931-32
Lide, Martha		A.B.	Intermediate Dept.; Mathematics	1922-23
Lide, Mary Frances		A.B.	Latin; French	1919-22
Lineberry, Annie Ruth		A.B.	Mathematics; Science	1923-24
Long, John Worth	Director of Public Relations	B.A.; B.D.	Speech	1953-54
Lovelace, A. C.	President	A.B.; M.Ed.		1935-36
Lovelace, Acquilla (See Mrs. F. B. Hamrick)				
Lovelace, Mrs. G. B.				
Lovelace, James Louis	Bursar	A.B.	Assistant in Music	1924-26
Lynch, W. C.		A.B.; Th.M.	Science; Bible	1923-25; 1938-45
Lytton, Evelyn		B.S.	Bible	1929-32
McAlister, Clyde Furman	Bursar	B.S.	Home Economics	1947-48
McAlister, Mrs. Clyde Furman		A.B.	English	1946-49
McBrayer, John Albert		B.S.	English	Fall 1947
McBrayer, Rinda Goode		A.B.	Mathematics	Spring 1948
McCown, Ruth		B.S.	Commercial	1931-41
McGee, Lula	Lady Principal	B.S.	Household Arts	1928-29
McLain, Mildred				1907-08
				1908-09
McMurtry, Rosalie	Librarian; Dean of Women	B.S.	Physical Education; Health; Library Science	1931-35
McPherson, Holt		B.A.	Journalism	1944-47
McSwain, Faye	Dietitian			1945-47

FACULTY AND ADMINISTRATIVE PERSONNEL (cont'd)

Name	Office	Degree	Subject Taught	Year
Marsh, Roy A.		A.B.	English; Latin	1913-14
Martin, Avarie M.		A.B.	History	1919-22
Martin, Santford, Jr.	Publicity Director	B.A.; M.A.	English	1948-51
Miller, Mrs. Santford, Jr.			Typing	Fall 1948
Moore, Abbie Catherine		B.M.; M.M.	Piano; Theory	1937-54; 1955-56
Moore, Dan W., Jr.		B.S.	Physical Education; Science	1939-41
Moore, Leila		A.B.	Art; China Painting	1919-22
Moore, Ollie		A.B.	Intermediate Dept.	1918-19
Moore, W. G.		A.B.; M.A.; B.D.	Bible	1919-22
Morgan, Mrs. James P.	Dean of Women	B.S.; M.S.	Religious Education	1943-44
Morgan, Saranan		B.S.	Physical Education; Health	1948-55
Morris, Lela		A.B.	Assistant in Music	1920-24
Morris, Mary			Household Arts and Science	1922-24
Morrisett, James Stephen	Head, Department of Religion	B.A.; M.A.	Religion; Choir; Greek	1945-55
Moseley, M. A., Jr.		B.S.; M.S.	Chemistry	1950-56
Mull, Nettie Earl	Dean of Women	A.B.	Science	1935-36
Odom, Janie Belle	Dietitian			1948-53; 1955-56
Osborne, J. W.			Business Law	Spring 1956
Pangle, Maxwell Galbraith		A.B; A.M.	Social Science	1929-34
Pangle, Mrs. Maxwell Galbraith		A.B.; A.M.	Mathematics	1929-34
Pangle, Jessie T. (See Mrs. O. P. Hamrick)				

FACULTY AND ADMINISTRATIVE PERSONNEL (cont'd)

Name	Office	Subject Taught	Degree	Year
Page, Ilma Johnson		Home Economics	B.S.; A.M.	1937-39
Patton, Pauline		Assistant in Music		1926-27
Paul, Fannie E.		Piano		1929-30
Pitts, Mary Clarke		Director of Music	B.M.	1907-09; 1915-16
Plaster, Mrs. Hubert S.		Organ	B.M.	1953-56
Plybon, Mrs. Louise Moore	Librarian		B.S.; B.S.L.S.; M.S.L.S.	1953-54
Pollock, Mrs. John Mark		Modern Languages	B.A.; M.A.	1936-56
Powell, Ruth Elaine		Home Economics	B.S.	1945-46
Powers, H. D.		Science	A.B.	1920-22
Propst, Mrs. Roy	Bursar			1943-46
Quinn, Mabel		Music		1917-23
Rackley, B. G.		Physical Education; Mathematics; Science	B.S.	1929-32
Rackley, Mrs. B. G.		Languages	B.A.; M.A.	1929-32
Radcliffe, Margaret C.		Music	B.A.; M.M.	1913-15
Raines, Mrs. Carroll		Physical Education; Health	B.S.	1946-48
Reece, Thomas L.		Religious Education	B.A.; B.D.	1947-48
Reese, Martha		Science	B.S.; M.A.	1928-30
Rice, Richard M.		Physical Education; Science	B.S.	1936-39
Richardson, Frank C.	Bursar	Commercial	B.S.	1950-53
Ritch, Mrs. Lillian M.	Dietitian			1915-44
Roberts, John Elgin, Jr.	Associate Director, Public Relations	English; Journalism	B.A.; M.A.	1954-56

FACULTY AND ADMINISTRATIVE PERSONNEL (cont'd)

Name	Office	Degree	Subject Taught	Year
Rodgers, Bessie			Assistant in Music; Art	1912-13
Rushing, H. C.		B.M.	Voice	1929-30
Sholar, Nell			Assistant in Music; Primary Dept.	1914-15
Shytle, Mrs. J. D.	Counselor for Boys		Physical Education; Science	1950-56
Simmons, Broadus E.		B.S.	Science	1929-31
Sink, Mrs. Maxwell		B.S.	Home Economics	1952-53
Smith, Alma		A.B.	English; Latin; History	1907-09
Smith, Dorothy Myers		A.B.	Physical Education	1943-45
Smith, Jennie		A.B.; A.M.	Social Science	1937-46
Smith, Shirley		B.M.	Violin	1948-49
Snuggs, H. L.		A.B.; M.A.	Modern Languages	1928-29
Spann, Liza		A.B.; M.A.	Science	1929-31
Spratt, Robert		B.S.	Band Instructor	1939-40
Stacy, Paul J.		A.B.	Natural Science	1941-56
Starnes, Mabel	Dean of Women		Speech	1950-56
Sullivan, Charlton Holmes	Dean of Instruction	B.A.; M.A.	Mathematics	1944-45
Swope, L. W.		M.A.; Th.M.	Bible	1917-19
Swope, Mrs. L. W.			Intermediate Dept.	1917-18
Taylor, Mary Gertrude			Commercial	1941-42
Terrell, James Orville	Dean of Instruction	B.S.; M.S.	Social Science	1945-56
Tillery, Mary H.			Art, China Painting; French	1922-25
Trentham, S. O.		B.S.; M.S.	Natural Science	1947-49

Name	Office	Degree	Subject Taught	Year
Trentham, Mrs. S. O.		B.A.; M.A.	Social Science	1947-49
Troutman, William F.	Head, Social Science Dept.	B.S.; M.A.	Social Science	1949-51; 1952-56
Vosecky, Eugene W.	Acting Bursar	B.S.; M.A.	Business Administration	1949-55
Wall, Zeno	President	D.D.		1930-32
Wallace, Mrs. Irma P.			Intermediate Dept.	1920-22
Walser, Patsy A.			Music	1916-17
Washburn, W. Wyan	College Physician	B.S.; M.D.	Journalism	1937-40; 1946-56
Watkins, Lilla E.		B.A.; M.A.	Commercial	1942-52
Watson, Euphenia			Art	1914-17
Welchel, Edward S.		AB; Th.M.; Th.D.	Bible	1932-36
Wells, H. H., Jr.		A.B.	Bible; Science; Mathematics	1924-26
Williams, Milton A.	Dean of Instruction	B.S.; M.A.	Science	1932-34
Wilson, T. L.			Commercial	1910-12
Withrow, Cleo		B.S.; M.A.	Home Economics	1950-52
Wofford, Ethel		A.B.	Primary and Intermediate Depts.	1915-20
Wood, Loyd T.		A.B.	Science; History	1925-27
Woody, Lorene			Music	1927-29
Wordragen, Jan Van			Music	1909-10
Wray, Carolyn L.	Librarian	B.A.; A.B.L.S.	Library Science; Latin; English	1943-53
Wray, Mrs. Joe S.			Latin	1946-50
Young, Richard L., Jr.	Counselor for Boys	B.A.	Journalism	1947-48

Those having served 20 years or more:

Mrs. Lillian M. Ritch — 29 years
Miss Etta L. Curtis — 27 years
Mr. J. D. Huggins — 24 years
Mr. O. P. Hamrick — 22 years
Mrs. Elma Harper Pollock — 20 years

Those having served 10 years or more:

Mrs. J. D. Huggins — 19 years
Mr. H. C. Dixon — 19 years
Miss Abbie Miller — 18 years
Mr. Paul J. Stacy — 15 years
Dr. P. L. Elliott — 13 years
Dr. T. C. Holland — 13 years
Dr. W. Wyan Washburn — 13 years
Rev. J. L. Jenkins — 12 years
Mr. J. O. Terrell — 11 years
Mr. J. Y. Hamrick — 11 years
Mr. L. A. Allen — 11 years
Mrs. Rinda Goode McBrayer — 10 years
Dr. Robert A. Dyer — 10 years
Mr. J. Stephen Morrisett — 10 years
Miss Carolyn Wray — 10 years
Miss Lilla Watkins — 10 years
Mrs. Dorothy W. Hamrick — 10 years

Appendix C

BOARD OF TRUSTEES

Hawkins, P. C.—1925-29
Haynes, R. R.—1910-11
Hendrick, Maurice—1941-43
Hicks, Walter L.—1929-50
Hildebrand, S. Bruce—1954-***
Hinson, Claude S.—1947-51;
   1953-56
**Holland, T. M.—1905-29
Hord, D. F.—1921-40
Horne, Ray—1941-44
Hudson, Rev. E. V.—1931-32;
   1945-46
Hudson, W. Hill, Sr.—1937-47
Huggins, Rev. Hubert—1945-46
Hunnicutt, Rev. J. A.—1932-38
Hunt, Rev. D. J.—1921-25
*Irvin, Rev. A. C.—1904-05;
   1908-09
Irvin, C. J.—1938-39
Irvin, J. Y.—1908-25
Jenkins, Rev. C. A.—1911-12
*Jenkins, L. S.—1904-05
Jessup, Rev. L. L.—1931-34
Jolley, A. I.—1915-37
Jolley, R. N.—1939-41
Jones, J. B.—1926-28
Jones, Rev. J. W.—1936-37
Keeter, Byron—1941-47
Keeter, D. J.—1918-32
*Kendrick, G. W.—1904-05
*Kendrick, N. B.—1904-32
Kincaid, Arnold W.—1950-56
King, Rev. T. H.—1922-24
Knox, Rev. Lattie—1934-35
Lamm, Rev. S. L.—1947-50
Lancaster, A. D.—1921-25
Lancaster, Rev. O. B.—1938-39
Lattimore, Walter S.—1911-15
Lawrence, Rev. Tom S.—
   1955-***
Lawrence, Rev. John E.—
   1956-***
Lee, Mrs. Norman B.—1940-44;
   1949-53
Lewis, R. S.—1924-32
*Logan, G. H.—1904-18
Long, Captain T. T.—1936-46
Lovelace, A. C.—1932-34
**Lovelace, Dr. T. B.—1905-13
Lovelace, Mrs. T. C.—1941-46
Lutz, J. F.—1935-44
**McBrayer, J. E.—1905-06
McBrayer, John Z.—1949-53
McCluney, Rev. J. L.—1944-46
McEntire, W. R.—1932-34
McKinney, A. M.—1932-39
McMurry, A. W.—1936-50

McMurry, Mrs. S.A.—1941-44
Maddrey, Rev. Charles A.—
   1934-36
Martin, Santford, Sr.—1950-55
**Martin, W. A.—1905-20
Matheney, Rev. C. C.—1925-32;
   1944-46
Matheny, J. A.—1938-39
Miller, Rev. J. R.—1915-17
**Moore, J. F.—1905-54 (Life
   Member)
Moore, John—1955-***
Moore, Rev. O. D.—1943-44
*Mull, A. T.—1904-05
Mull, O. M.—1941-46
Owens, Rev. M. O., Jr.—1954-***
Owens, J. E.—1946-50
Padgett, James—1950-54
Padgett, Rev. Rush—1929-31
Padgett, Mrs. T. R.—1941-48
Parris, Rev. T. H.—1936-39
Parsons, Rev Joe—1941-43
Payseur, Rev. C. W.—1911-12
Pettit, Rev. W. E.—1944-50
Pinnix, L. C.—1946-47
Plaster, Dr. Hubert S.—1955-***
Plybon, Rev. Charles T.—1934-37
Potter, Rev. James S.—1947-52
Price, L. C.—1939-43
Price, R. E.—1941-48; 1951-55
Price, U. R.—1936-37
Pruett, G. B.—1909-34
*Putnam, Rev. D. F.—1904-06;
   1922-25
**Putnam, J. D.—1905-21
Putnam, J. L.—1921-32
Quinn, Aaron B.—1941-50
*Quinn, J. H.—1904-38
Ray, Rev. James—1945-46
Reece, R. P.—1954-***
Riddle, W. F.—1924-25
Ridings, C. O.—1937-38
Rimmer, Rev. W. W.—1929-31
Roberts, Guy H.—1945-50;
   1953-56
Rollins, Howard—1955-56
Rollins, J. U.—1929-48; 1950-56
Royster, H. C.—1929-32
Royster, D. W., Sr.—1955-***
Sargeant, Rev. A. G.—1941-43
Self, Hattie Peeler (Mrs. L. L.)—
   1950-***
**Sims, Rev. A. H.—1905-07
Smith, Yates—1944-46
Spangler, A. D.—1925-29
Spangler, C. D.—1953-56
Spangler, Mal A.—1936-47

Sperling, Mrs. E. G.—1939-44
Stamey, T. A.—1920-29
Stembridge, Dr. H. Hansel, Jr.—
1952-55
Stoudemire, Rev. A. T.—1928-31
Stout, Carson—1952-56
Stowe, D. P.—1926-32
Strickland, Rev. B. M.—1939-46
Stroup, M. A.—1920-21
Stroup, A. U.—1922-31
Stroup, Mrs. Rush—1934-39;
1941-46; 1948-53; (1954-***
Treasurer)
Summey, T. S.—1945-46
Suttle, J. L., Jr.—1955-***
Suttle, Rev. John W.—1911-
(Life Member)
Tarlton, Rev. W. V.—1943-46
Tarlton, J. J.—1944-47
Tate, Rev. W. T.—1919-26
Taylor, Rev. J. Ned—1945-46
Tew, Rev. C. T.—1911-14
Toms, W. A.—1938-41
Vann, J. G.—1948-51
Vipperman, Dr. J. L.—1922-24
Wacaster, Mrs. John—1932-44
Walker, Z. R.—1931-32
Wall, Dr. Zeno—1928-39; 1941-46
Walters, W. L.—1924-32
Washburn, A. V., Sr.—1927-28;
1954-***
Washburn, George—1941-46
Washburn, Joe C.—1934-46
*Washburn, W. W.—1904-33
Washburn, Dr. W. Wyan—
1946-***
Weathers, Lee B.—1950-55
**Weathers, R. L.—1905-11
Webb, Judge E. Y.—1936-45;
1951-55
Webb, Selma—1941-50
Weekley, Rev. H. Gordon, Jr.—
1954-***
Whitaker, D. C.—1938-39
Whitaker, E. G.—1941-46
White, Rev. E. P.—1936-37
White, Rev. Harold—1955-***
Whitley, Rev. J. W.—1926-32
Williams, W. W.—1925-26
Wilson, C. B.—1921-29
*Wilson, J. M.—1904-08
Withrow, J. P. D.—1909-11
Woodward, Joe Lee—1940-46
Yelton, Mrs. Paris L.—1946-48;
1950-54
Young, Carlos—1953-56
Young, Margaret—1941-50

———
* On original board appointed in
1904 for Kings Mountain Asso-
ciation
** On joint board appointed in
1905 for Kings Mountain and
Sandy Run Associations
*** Currently serving on board

Those having served 40 years or
more:
Mr. J. F. Moore	49 yrs.
(Life Member)	
Rev. J. W. Suttle	45+ yrs.
(Life Member)	
Mr. E. B. Hamrick	44 yrs.
(Life Members)	

Those having served 30 years or
more:
Mr. B. T. Falls, Sr.	35 yrs.
Mr. J. H. Quinn	33 yrs.

Those having served 20 years or
more:
Mr. W. W. Washburn	29 yrs.
Mr. J. J. Edwards	28 yrs.
Mr. N. B. Kendrick	28 yrs.
Mr. G. B. Pruett	25 yrs.
Mr. J. U. Rollins	25 yrs.
Mr. D. M. Harrill	24 yrs.
Mr. T. M. Holland	24 yrs.
Mr. A. I. Jolley	22 yrs.
Mr. W. L. Hicks	21 yrs.

Those having served 10 years or
more:
Mr. D. F. Hord	19 yrs.
Mr. E. C. Borders	18 yrs.
Mr. Carme Elam	18 yrs.
Mrs. Rush Stroup	17 yrs.
Mr. J. Y. Irvin	17 yrs.
Mr. L. S. Hamrick	16 yrs.
Mr. J. D. Putnam	16 yrs.
Rev. Zeno Wall	16 yrs.
Dr. W. A. Ayers	15 yrs.
Mr. W. A. Martin	15 yrs.
Mr. M. M. Green	14 yrs.
Mr. C. E. Hamrick	14 yrs.
Mr. D. J. Keeter	14 yrs.
Mr. G. H. Logan	14 yrs.
Mr. A. W. McMurry	14 yrs.
Rev. J. J. Beach	13 yrs.
Judge E. Y. Webb	13 yrs.
Mrs. John Wacaster	12 yrs.
Mr. J. C. Washburn	12 yrs.
Mr. J. R. Dover, Jr.	11 yrs.
Mr. George M. Gold	11 yrs.

Mr. R. E. Price	11 yrs.	Mr. W. J. Francis	10 yrs.
Mr. J. L. Putnam	11 yrs.	Mr. S. H. Hamrick	10 yrs.
Mr. Mal A. Spangler	11 yrs.	Mr. G. V. Hawkins	10 yrs.
Mr. J. R. Walker	11 yrs.	Mr. W. Hill Hudson, Sr.	10 yrs.
Rev. J. A. Brock	10 yrs.	Captain T. T. Long	10 yrs.
Mr. R. F. Craig	10 yrs.	Dr. W. Wyan Washburn	10 yrs.

Appendix D

ENROLLMENT

1907-08 — 135	
1908-09 — 219	
1909-10 — 172	
1910-11 — 268	
1911-12 — 229	
1912-13 — 170	
1913-14 — 209	
1914-15 — 234	
1915-16 — 259	
1916-17 — 240	
1917-18 — 272	
1918-19 — 315	
1919-20 — 366	
1920-21 — 309	
1921-22 — 273	
1922-23 — 269	
1923-24 — 287	
1924-25 — 272	
1925-26 — 224	
1926-27 — 184	
1927-28 — 138	
1928-29 — 237	(61C; 176 HS)
1929-30 — 214	(109C; 105 HS)
1930-31 — 221	(98C; 123 HS)
1931-32 — 155	(76C; 79 HS)
1932-33 — 224	(109C; 115 HS)
1933-34 — 227	(89C; 138 HS)

1934-35 — 114		
1935-36 — 140		
1936-37 — 143		
1937-38 — 225		
1938-39 — 218		
1939-40 — 166		
1940-41 — 130		
1941-42 — 106		
1942-43 — 169		
1943-44 — 164	Summer School	
1944-45 — 234	—	13
1945-46 — 306	—	90
1946-47 — 420	—	80
1947-48 — 410	—	91
1948-49 — 420	—	113
1949-50 — 453	—	91
1950-51 — 397	—	77
1951-52 — 393	—	62
1952-53 — 421	—	58
1953-54 — 369	—	78
1954-55 — 413	—	117
1955-56 — 473	—	98

Total High School Enrollment: 5,780
Total College Enrollment: 7,794

GRAND TOTAL: 13,574

Appendix E
GRADUATES

High School		College		
1910 — 6		1930 — 37		
1911 — 5		1931 — 33		
1912 — 10		1932 — 16		
1913 — 16		1933 — 34		
1914 — 13		1934 — 37		
1915 — 18		1935 — 32		
1916 — 20		1936 — 51		
1917 — 17		1937 — 27		
1918 — 30		1938 — 35		
1919 — 22		1939 — 52		
1920 — 24		1940 — 29		
1921 — 45		1941 — 28		
1922 — 30		1942 — 20		
1923 — 60		1943 — 26		
1924 — 64		1944 — 34		
1925 — 62		1945 — 32		
1926 — 53		1946 — 37		
1927 — 46		1947 — 65		
1928 — 47		1948 — 81	(Spring: 71; Summer: 10)	
1929 — 31		1949 — 101	(Spring: 77; Summer: 24)	
1930 — 27		1950 — 113	(Spring: 97; Summer: 16)	
1931 — 19*		1951 — 96	(Spring: 88; Summer: 8)	
1932 — 17		1952 — 91	(Spring: 88; Summer: 3)	
1933 — 15		1953 — 75	(Spring: 70; Summer: 5)	
1934 — 18		1954 — 80	(Spring: 72; Summer: 8)	
—		1955 — 76	(Spring: 66; Summer: 10)	
Total: 715		1956 — 77	(Spring: 68; Summer: 9)	

* Joint operation by State and   Total: 1,415
Boiling Springs Junior
College

GRAND TOTAL: High School and College: 2,130

Index

213

214   INDEX

Education, Committee on, Kings Mountain Association, 19, 22, 26, 73, 114
Edward VIII, King of England, 91-92
Edwards, Carl, 30
Edwards, J. J., 23
Elam, Carme, 20, 23, 50
Elliott, Dathia, 130, 147
Elliott, Dr. Philip Lovin, x, xi, xiv, 98-100, 101, 107, 113, 114-115, 117, 118, 119, 124, 127, 129, 134, 135, 136-137, 139, 143, 146, 150, 151-152, 153, 159, 160, 162, 163, 164, 165, 166, 168, 169, 170, 171, 172, 174, 175, 176, 177, 178; accepted presidency, 99; inaugurated, 102-105
Elliott, Mrs. Philip Lovin, 99, 139
Elliott, Lizzie, 25
Elliott, Dr. Robert N., Jr., 177
Elizabeth Baptist Church, 52, 53, 87
Emerson, Ralph Waldo, quoted, xi
Endowment, 69, 87, 118, 119, 169, 171
English, George L., 53
Enrollment, 67, 71, 72, 169, 171
Ervin, Sam J., Jr., 174
Erwin, Dr. Clyde A., 79
Executive Committee, Board of Trustees, 62, 76, 77, 85, 99, 100, 101, 102, 105, 106, 113, 114, 116, 117, 118, 124, 125, 128, 134, 170
Ewing, C. Meade, 56

Faculty, xvi, 67, 73, 74, 76, 77, 79, 82, 116, 117, 142, 160, 166, 167-168, 169, 175-176, 178
Falls, B. T., 26, 68, 78
Farm, The Gardner-Webb College Miracle, 106-107, 114, 146-151, 152, 159-160, 165
Farrar, Rev. John S., 161
Farris, T. N., 32, 39, 42, 45
Felton, Ralph A., 154
Fisher, Benjamin Coleman, 128-129, 129-130, 130-131, 132, 133, 134, 138, 153, 154, 161, 163, 164-165, 166
Football, 57-58, 72, 73, 75, 161
Ford Foundation Gift, 174-175
Francis, William J., 46, 48, 49

Gaddy, Claude F., 161
Gamble, Mrs. J. Warren, 133
Gardner Foundation, 124-125, 136, 137, 140, 172

Gardner, James Webb "Decker", 88-89, 120, 140
Gardner, Oliver Harry, 121
Gardner, Governor O. Max, ix, xi, 88, 90, 91, 93, 94, 97, 98, 100, 101, 102, 103, 105, 113, 114, 115, 116, 120, 125, 132, 137, 138, 142, 150, 163, 168; gave $10,000 for scholarships, 89; suggested New Deal to Roosevelt, 90-91; wrote letter to survey committee, 94-96; purchased Gardner - Webb College farm, 106; appointed Ambassador to the Court of St. James, 121-123; died, 123-124
Gardner, Mrs. O. Max, 91, 124, 136, 136-137, 139, 172
Gardner, O. Max, Jr., 88-89, 124, 125, 129, 136, 137, 172
Gardner, O. Max, Memorial Student Center, 124, 136-137, 138, 150, 161, 169
Gardner, Ralph Webb, 88-89, 124, 133, 137, 165, 172
Gardner-Webb College, xi, xvi, 20, 94, 96, 97, 99, 103, 107, 113, 115, 116, 117, 118, 119, 120, 122, 123, 125, 126, 127, 128, 130, 131, 132, 133, 134, 135, 136, 138, 140, 142, 146, 150, 157, 164, 165, 166, 168; Community-Service concept, xiv-xvi, 175; named for Gardner and Webb families, 94; Charter changed, 118, 119
Gardner-Webb College Recreation Center, xiv, 170, 171, 178
Gardner-Webb Community Health Center, xiv, 114, 143-146, 159, 165, 169, 174
Gardner-Webb Endowment Fund Campaign, 119, 120, 121, 128-129, 130, 132, 134, 135, 138, 164
Gaston Baptist Association, 58, 61, 62, 64, 72, 73, 76; given ten members on the Board of Trustees, 58
G. I. Apartments, 120
Glenn, George P., 50
Gold, Maude, 33, 39
Golden Anniversary Year, xi, 170-172, 173-174
Goode, Rev. J. M., 53, 54
Goode, Tommy, 30
Graham, Dr. Frank Porter, 94, 147; delivered inaugural address of President Elliott, 104-105

junior college. As a junior college, it weathered the Great Depression — those bleak, depression-ridden years of the '30's when the institution was kept alive through the dogged determination, faith, and sacrifice of faithful friends.

Two significant things in the life of the College occurred in 1942—Governor O. Max Gardner began to devote his energies, time, and wealth to guiding and strengthening the College; and the name of the College was changed to Gardner-Webb College. In July of the next year, 1943, another significant event in the history of the school occurred—Phil Elliott came to Gardner-Webb as its President, bringing with him a community-service concept of education that has made Gardner-Webb somewhat unique among small liberal arts colleges.

In 1949, Senator Clyde R. Hoey declared that "the history of this institution with its early struggle for existence as Boiling Springs Junior College and its rebirth when it became Gardner-Webb College reads like a romance." That "romance" is told in LENGTHENED SHADOWS: A HISTORY OF GARDNER-WEBB COLLEGE, 1907-1956.

ATHLETIC FIELD

GAFFNEY ROAD

· SCALE · IN · FEET ·

100   0   100